Praise for the Book

"As I read Don's book, I kept saying, 'Yes!' *Yes* to his complete understanding of and sensitivity to the challenges of church governance; *yes* to his articulation of the Biblical story as it relates to our discernment work together; and *yes* to the inclusion of both leadership and business best practices. Don Zimmer's writing, weaving the personal, theological, and practical together, invites us to engage our imaginations as we listen with open minds, hearts, and wills to God's yearnings for us."
—*Ruth D. Anderson, Executive Director,*
The Servant Leadership School of Greensboro

"How does God speak to and through a church's governing board? Where is the proper place for *Robert's Rules of Order* to intersect with the mission of Jesus Christ in the world, the Bible, and prayer? Donald E. Zimmer builds upon years of path-finding research and church experience to chart a course for church institutions to discover God's desires and to deepen the spiritual life, vitality, and mission of the congregation."
—*Wendy J. Deichmann, president, United Theological Seminary*

"Don Zimmer offers a model for church leadership in the 21st century. The model rests on church boards listening to God first through grounding in spiritual practices. Church leaders interested in living into the potential God offers churches, rather than maintaining structures, will find this book essential reading."
—*Valerie Isenhower, Executive Director, Water in the Desert Ministries*

"Like Luke the physician, whose medical background informs his Gospel, Don Zimmer weds corporate governance and business leadership models with spiritual formation practices to invite church leaders into the laboratory of spiritual discernment. He distills a wide range of scientific and spiritual wisdom with practical transformative depth."

—*Kent Ira Groff, founding mentor of Oasis Ministries for Spiritual Development and author of* Active Spirituality: A Guide for Seekers and Ministers *and* Facing East, Praying West: Poetic Reflections on the Spiritual Exercises.

"In a world filled with much well intentioned noise, quiet and listening can easily get lost. Don lays out a radical proposition: What if the church listened to God, nature, and one another in order to more fully learn what it means to be church today? A beautiful, thoughtful approach for those within the church with the courage to revisit what is in order to see what might be."

—*Joseph B. Judge, president, Clear Possibilities, LLC*

"Don Zimmer draws from his vast reading and experience in writing this transformational book. He invites us to re-imagine church governance by challenging us to move from our corporate, culture-driven model to a community led by the Spirit. To do this he urges us to steward the church by listening to God and to our neighbors."

—*Rev. Arthur Umbach, Mission & Ministry Facilitator and Director of Spiritual Life, Southeastern District, Lutheran Church-Missouri Synod*

Leadership and Listening

Leadership and Listening

Spiritual Foundations for Church Governance

DONALD E. ZIMMER

Herndon, Virginia
www.alban.org

The Alban Institute
2121 Cooperative Way, Suite 100
Herndon, VA 20171

Cover design by Tobias Becker, BirdBox Design.

Library of Congress Cataloging-in-Publication Data

Zimmer, Donald E., 1938-
  Leadership and listening : spiritual foundations for church governance / Donald E. Zimmer.
    p. cm.
  Includes bibliographical references (p. 177).
  ISBN 978-1-56699-414-9
  1. Church polity. 1. Title.
  BV647.3.Z56 2011
  262--dc22

                        2011014437

11   12   13   14   15   VP   5   4   3   2   1

Contents

Foreword

A CALL FROM SHELBY ANDRESS BACK IN THE MID-nineties grabbed my attention. She said, "Chuck, you need to know Don Zimmer. He will be attuned to the work you are doing." Shelby was an evaluator for a number of projects which the Lilly Endowment was funding on not-for-profit board development and knew of my research and work to integrate spirituality in governance on church boards. Her introduction initiated a relationship of mutual respect, friendship, and common interests focused on what does or does not happen at church board and council meetings. Our journey together has encompassed strategizing for leadership development, listening for the presence and spirit of the Holy, enjoying a birthday ride in the Colorado mountains, sharing family stories, comparing chemotherapy hopes and fears, and now—writing another book.

Don is uniquely suited to write this book. When the Worshipful-Work board chose him to do "the work" of sifting a decade of its initiatives and learnings in spirituality and discernment, he became the steward of an important ministry and its legacy—all with an eye to offering it to the church for its ongoing discerning process. He has added his own lifetime of personal journey through church boards and a wealth of knowledge from published literature in the field. Leadership exploration groups in which we both participated always were in awe of the vast scope of the publications he cited. The song from the musical, *The Music Man*, affirms, "You gotta know the territory." And Don knows it inside and out!

Early in the life of Worshipful-Work, founded in 1995 on the heels of the Lilly funded church board project, it became apparent that the called for change in church board culture could not be a one-, two-, or three-year program or initiative. It would need to be on the front burner of the church's attention for at least a decade. Now that the decade has passed, we are even more aware that a monumental shift in its culture needs to be rearticulated by a chorus of voices over and over again for a number of decades. The current business and western parliamentary culture is so deeply ingrained and familiar that potential shifts are directly resisted or ignored. People tend to keep on doing what they know how to do. Don accesses the voices of a host of folks who tasted and saw a new and vital way forward. Their voices are now able to echo into the ears of a new generation of church leaders who yearn for a way to integrate spirituality into the agendas of their meetings.

And I want to extend a word of appreciation and affirmation to the staff of the Alban Institute for their willingness to continue to put this important message before the church. Loren Mead, its founder, outlined his vision for an initiative to care about congregations as an evangelism strategy on a napkin to me over coffee back in Atlanta in the late '60s. So when I finished the manuscript for *Transforming Church Boards into Communities of Spiritual Leaders* back in 1994, I went back to them to explore its publication. Celia Hahn, their editor for publications, submitted it to an advisory panel, which advised against its publication on the basis that it introduced the vocabulary of "spirituality." Spirituality had not been an emphasis of Alban to that date. Celia overrode their advice because she was noticing an increasing number of publications on that exact subject. The book had named the tendency to rely on business and organizational development models for board formation and functioning—and called for the introduction of spiritual practice in the conduct of meetings. Thanks to Celia's "discernment" and courage, it became one of Alban's all time best sellers.

Jim Wind, Alban's current president, was the program officer at Lilly who oversaw and guided me in the church board project back in the early 1990s. His influence and encouragement continue to come home to the Institute. Since the publication of *Transforming Church Boards*, Alban has continued to add to a stable of books that affirm and explore the place of spiritual practice and presence. Don's work expands and probes deeper into the meaning and place of spirituality in leadership and administration. This book is actually a narrative account of a seventeen-year journey of the Worshipful-Work's initiative that has influenced a number of folks. It is also the story of folks like Don, who have influenced and shaped the effort. (So it is also a good fit for Alban's recent venture into narrative leadership.) Alban is to be commended for keeping this important theme alive in the church decade after decade. It is now part of Alban's congregational leadership DNA!

Charles M. Olsen

Preface

BETWEEN 1992 AND 1996 I HAD THE OPPORTUNITY TO BE A part of a number of leadership development programs at the Center for Creative Leadership in Greensboro, North Carolina. Spirituality was just finding its way into the Center's curriculum by way of experiences designed to explore the implications of quantum physics for leadership and organization. I encountered a host of ideas, which in my naivete I associated exclusively with Eastern and Native American religious practices and the New Age movement. I remember returning home from one of the weeklong sessions I attended with twenty other nonprofit executives with the question: If spirituality is as important as it appears to be, where is the Christian voice? Why was the Christian voice not included in these critical conversations about leadership? Were we willing to cede to these other voices what was obviously becoming an important topic for senior executives of the corporations that are such a big part of our society? I was not. Surely Christianity has something to say about leadership and the behavior of organizations beyond proselytizing, which data shows is clearly unwelcome in the workplace. It turns out that Christianity does have something to say, but it was securely out of my field of view and that of most of my contemporaries. The roots of this book go back to that experience. The rest of the story of my efforts to understand spirituality and explore its importance to church governance surfaces in the chapters that follow.

The list of people who have encouraged, enabled, challenged, and equipped me for this journey is long. By the time I first attended a Center for Creative Leadership program, four pastors had already opened doors that made it possible for me to be at the Center in the first place. Jim De Lange modeled church governance rooted in relationships and emphasized the need for the church to engage the world rather than retreat from it. Bob Johnson invited me to join a small group experience that helped me gain valuable insights into authentic Christian community. Eric Peterson opened the doors to the quarter-century relationship with the biblical text that grounds this work. Rich Hinz made it possible to experience the best leadership development programs in the country and first introduced me to servant leadership.

Soon after my experiences at the Center for Creative Leadership, I met Chuck Olsen. He introduced me to the connection between spirituality and governance and later extended the invitation to join the board of Worshipful-Work. Dave Travis and Linda Stanley enabled me to experience the community of megachurches clustered around Leadership Network and be exposed to the leading minds in the world of leadership and organization. The members of the Worshipful-Work board—Kathryn Damiano, Steve Doughty, Eileen Goor, Jerry Haas, Tara Hornbecker, Charles Tollett, and Connie Wilson—encouraged me to pursue a doctor of ministry program focused on spirituality and governance, gave me permission to use the resources of Worshipful-Work for my dissertation, and championed me through the process. Together we explored how to make corporate spiritual discernment the centerpiece of church governance.

This book would never even have been possible had not United Theological Seminary in Dayton, Ohio, been willing to accept a nonordained person into their Doctor of Ministry program and gone out of their way to help me take the prerequisite courses I needed when I needed them. My mentors at United—Jay McDaniel, Jane-Ann Clarke, David Clarke, Young Lee Hertig, and Paul Knitter—offered me the freedom and encouragement to explore, shared their wisdom, and challenged my perspectives. And my peer group—Deb Clark, Karla Kauffman, and Lynette Reed—faithfully companioned me throughout the research and writing phases of my dissertation. Judy Brown, Beverly Winterscheid, Ruth Anderson, and Michael Glaser were generous with their time and very helpful in a whole variety of ways as I sought to keep connected to the world of business and education. Marlene Lund, Marianne Latall, and Kathleen Glaser, each a teacher and school administrator, helped me to see leadership and governance with childlike eyes and understand the challenge of creating learning environments for people to grow.

Through it all, Bill Mockus, my spiritual director, has sought to keep me centered in prayer while maintaining a sense of humor. Daughters Andrea and Melissa, son Jeff, and grandson Corey have added to my sense of purpose and continually expanded my horizons. My wife of forty-eight years, Sherie, has been extraordinarily generous in her support, prayers, friendship, and unconditional love ever since she recovered from the shock of her sixty-six-year-old husband asking how she felt about him taking a portion of their retirement savings to return to school for a Doctor of Ministry degree. Editor Beth Ann Gaede has patiently guided me through the process of writing, gently nudging me to think in new ways and revisit my intuitions, and encouraging me along what has been an incredible spiritual journey.

Finally, seventy-eight people, most of whom I had never met, took time from their busy lives to talk with me on the phone and respond to a nine-question survey on spirituality and governance. Thirty-three others allowed me to listen to their conversations over a four-day period on the same subject. Their combined thoughts and experiences are the core of this research. Without them this work could not have gone forward. To each of you, thank you. You are a true blessing.

Introduction

The way the early disciples lived mystified people around them because the disciples seemed to live in another world. The principles that guided them clearly differed from those that guided others. They practiced a way of life both beautiful and mysterious. Their lives made sense only if one knew that they were living by the power and guidance of God. Their lives were governed by the reign of God and not by the press of politics or the call of culture. They were different because they chose to live their lives in obedience to and in the presence of God. Their radical love for God and neighbor resulted in dramatic actions that perplexed all who observed them (italics added).[1]

—RUEBEN P. JOB

OVER THE YEARS, RUEBEN JOB'S REFLECTIONS AS ELDER statesman, author, spiritual guide, and former bishop in the United Methodist Church have been a precious source of wisdom and support for many people seeking a deeper relationship with God in the midst of their service to the institutional church. His observations remind us that people who profess to be followers of Jesus are still called to live "in obedience to and in the presence of God" regardless of the context. The call to such a way of life mystifies many and challenges all. The goal of living in "obedience to and in the presence of God" is not to seek power, prosperity, or even survival but to know and respond lovingly to the desires of God's heart. Is it possible

1

for the church to live this way of life in the world today? Perhaps, but I believe it will require a reimagining of church leadership and the practice of governance and management so that the focus is first on stillness and listening to God together. Too often stillness and listening are sacrificed for action—action typically focused on developing and managing programs, people, financial resources, and facilities. Action is necessary, but it must be rooted in the desires of God.

There is considerable evidence that many church boards, especially those in congregations, are not healthy. A number of authors, among them John Ackerman, Diana Butler Bass, Kent Ira Groff, Loren Mead, Chuck Olsen, Graham Standish, and Karen-Marie Yust, write of needed improvements. Among the evidence cited are limited horizons, archaic models, the tyranny of the immediate, overemphasis on business, conflict, unmet emotional needs, religious differences, inattention to personal and corporate spiritual growth, and countless inefficiencies. The participants in the research that serves as the foundation for this book continually cited an inability and unwillingness among board members to practice the disciplines of prayer and spiritual discernment together in board settings. All of these factors contribute to a governing board's health and its ability or inability to seek together God's desires and follow them.

Since it became Romanized in the fourth century, the Western church has been dominated by a culture of rational thought, hierarchical leadership, and an emphasis on management. Over the years, ideas adopted from European monarchy, canon law, parliamentary law, the Age of Enlightenment, Newtonian science, and the economic model that has accompanied the growth of corporations in the Western world have been layered on and woven into church culture. The result has been a long-standing symbiotic relationship between the church and the government and more recently between the church and the business world. As these relationships have developed, the requirement to efficiently manage resources and the press of day-to-day activity have squeezed out time for spiritual practices and relationship development within church governance and management and have eliminated much of what is meaningful in life from workplaces of the business world.

The contemporary church is rooted in both the kingdom of God and the systems and cultures of government and business. Most people who serve in governing and management roles in the church in the United States today have been formed in the corporate world and acculturated to the parliamentary process that shapes our participation in government. Much of the work that church boards oversee and churches administer is associated with membership, employee relations, financial resources, property, programs, and organizational and legal issues. As a result, managing the institutional church's affairs inevitably trumps developing a board's spiritual life, especially where time is scarce and board members have not been prepared to think differently. "Business" must be taken care of and should be well done. Unfortunately, too many church governing boards are too much about business and not enough about their primary task: discerning God's desires for the part of the church they serve. Boards are focused too narrowly, their horizons are too low, their time frame is too short, and their sense of identity and purpose too limited. John Ackerman, Presbyterian pastor, author, and spiritual director, lays out the problem well in *Listening to God: Spiritual Formation in the Congregation*:

> It is my experience that *few congregations listen to God's call* to them, and few help members to listen to their individual call and to nurture their ongoing relationship with God. . . . *Most congregations and people don't know how to listen to God.* Congregations make up their minds by voting according to *Robert's Rules of Order.* They rarely listen to God or to each other. Individuals may be doing all kinds of work for God, but they rarely stop long enough to hear what God might have in mind (italics added)[2]

I believe church leaders must fundamentally change the way they view leadership, governance, and management in their organizations if they are to take seriously the need to listen to God's desires before acting. Listening, however, is not easy. We live in a culture of action and accomplishment that emphasizes measurement, efficiency, growth, and short-term profitability. Being still and listening simply does not fit. Moving toward a board culture within the church that seeks first to listen is challenging, some might say impossible.

Michael Glaser, Maryland's poet laureate, speaks to the challenge in his poem, "Adam at Work."

> How can my mind,
> filled with the commerce of man,
> listen for the voices of angels?[3]

Considerable research suggests that a real desire to listen to something other than the noise of the "commerce of man" is emerging. Even the world of business is recognizing that it can no longer focus solely on efficiency, growth, and short-term profitability. More and more people in the business world are seeking meaning in their work, the opportunity to develop their giftedness in what they do, the assurance that their work contributes to the sustainability of creation, and the opportunity for others to enjoy the basics of life. A triple bottom line of profits, people, and planet is receiving increasing emphasis. My research suggests that both the church and the business community have an abundance of insight and resources that can help boards shift toward a focus on seeking first the desires of God's heart and then responding effectively. Church boards need only to look around and begin deciding, one day at a time; they need only to be still and listen to God together and then to act. When the oft-repeated words from Isaiah are spoken in our celebrations of the Savior's birth, the church needs to experience more than their warmth. We need to also hear the prophet's assurance that the anticipated Savior can actually be the foundation for our leadership and government.

> For to us a child is born,
>   to us a son is given,
> and the government will be on his shoulders.
>   And he will be called
> Wonderful Counselor, Mighty God,
>   Everlasting Father, Prince of Peace.
> Of the increase of his government and peace
>   there will be no end.
> He will reign on David's throne and over his kingdom,
>   establishing and upholding it

with justice and righteousness
    from that time on and forever.
The zeal of the LORD Almighty will accomplish this.
Is. 9:6–7 NIV

Too often, however, those people who can imagine a model of church governance and management grounded in Jesus do not participate in church governance and management, or, if they do participate, they do not try to reshape it. At the same time, those who do serve in church governance and management too often have difficulty imagining how grounding governance and management in Jesus might enable them to better manage church affairs. When I talk to board members about Isaiah 9:6–7, most are very skeptical of relying on something other than parliamentary process and traditional management practices. I frequently hear, "Nothing will ever get done." Others are willing to accept the possibility that it may be desirable to rely more on God but feel bound by existing systems and the overwhelming task of changing an institution like the church. One pastor, speaking for a group standing with him, once told me that his board didn't even have time to do the business of the congregation, let alone listen for God! I am not sure his statement came out the way he really meant it, but I suspect many others share the feelings he expressed.

When I survey meeting agendas of church boards, especially those in smaller congregations, and listen to what the people serving on them experience, it is not hard to see why shifting the primary focus from managing church resources toward listening to God is so difficult. Boards are filled with good people facing tough fiscal and programmatic realities. Their challenges range from keeping aging ships afloat to handling rapid growth, all with too little time and too few resources. Board members are typically ill-prepared for the challenges of listening to God together. Many have agreed to serve with no expectation of being involved in "spiritual stuff" and often see such work as someone else's responsibility. Too often boards lack the imagination, understanding, skills, time, and motivation to deal with issues that lie outside what they are used to, so they don't. They choose instead to fill their time together with the day-to-day business that is familiar to them. In the process, they experience the frustrations and conflict associated with uncentered living, and they diminish the life and mission of the church by robbing it of much of God's generosity.

A dear friend of mine was fond of saying, "First, you have to think it." Many of the complex human, religious, and environmental challenges all of us face in this world cannot be addressed using the processes and people that have brought us to this point. To be faithful to God's original mandate to be stewards of the world, to love God and our neighbor as ourselves, and to carry the gospel to the "ends of the earth," we in the church need to take a new yet ancient course. That course requires adopting a governing philosophy that emphasizes discerning and living out God's desire, modeling the servant leadership Jesus advocated, and transforming the board from a place of managing the daily affairs of the church to a place where listening prayer, worship, reflection, and community are the first priority.

Years ago I was introduced to a model adapted from business for use in church boards. It emphasized the importance of both task accomplishment and relationship development. The model made the point that a healthy board needs to be concerned with more than carrying on programs, increasing attendance, raising money, and maintaining buildings; relationships are also important. Today, businesses are learning that accomplishing tasks and developing relationships are no longer enough. Questions of meaning, once the domain of the church, are now being raised in the workplace. People in the church and the business world are all longing for something more than our existing models offer. *Spirituality* is the term often used to describe this yearning. Traditionally, *spirituality* has been a church term used to describe one's relationship with God. Today the term is so widely used in so many contexts that it requires definition. I use the term *spirituality* in this book to mean the common desire for wholeness that people in the church and in the business world say is missing from their corporate lives. In the church, spirituality typically refers to the desire for a deeper relationship with God rooted in spiritual disciplines, specifically discernment, prayer, biblical-theological reflection, and story sharing. In the business world, spirituality tends to mean the human desire to find meaning and develop one's gifts in the workplace. One of the great challenges in developing this book has been addressing the differences in how spirituality is understood across the church, the business world, and the larger culture. If we can somehow overcome the challenges of language, I believe the church can learn from the world of business how to be more effective when spirituality is integrated into governance and management, and business can learn from church board practices rooted in more intentional listening to God.

Too often we Christians who serve the church in roles of governance and management are content to live a bifurcated life. We embrace and proclaim a triune God whose essence is love; a God who is both creator and servant, who endured humiliation and death for us; and a God whose presence surrounds and fills us each moment. Yet we model our internal governance and management after earthly kingdoms and the business world, whose values are not centered in listening to and obeying God. In doing so, we exchange the power and creativity of the Spirit freely moving within our community for the control and predictability valued in the business world. Too often we have sought to "right" the power structures Jesus turned upside down and to bind the Spirit to our perceptions and comfort. The time has come to listen to voices from the church community calling for a greater reliance on listening to God and from the business community calling for greater meaning in the world of work.

This book began in the stories told by the men and women who participated in the 2006 gathering, "Discernment as Gracious Space: Sharing, Experiencing, and Exploring the Deep Joy of Communal Discernment," hosted by Worshipful-Work at the Upper Room in Nashville. It germinated in my reflections on my life experiences. My dissertation, "Listening to God: The Challenges of Deepening Spirituality in the Governing and Administrative Structures of Mainline Denominations" provided the soil for this book to take root and grow. In writing this book, I have sought to draw together relevant insights from a host of influences from the historic church and the world of business that converge in the contemporary church. Together they highlight the centrality of listening to God and offer a foundation for responding to the practical issues of living God's will into being in contemporary church governance and management settings. Finally, I present the insights that contemporary leaders who participated in this research have drawn from their efforts to help congregations, judicatories, and nonprofits more fully listen to God. This book also tells my own journey into imagining a different kind of church governance and management culture as I have sought to integrate the worlds of business, science, education, the church, and spirituality that have been a part of my life. My hope is that you will look at the way the governing boards on which you serve, beginning with your congregation, go about governing and administering themselves, so that listening to God together is their primary focus.

In his book *The Prophetic Imagination*, Walter Brueggemann, Old Testament scholar and author, contrasts two imaginations that he believes shape church life. The "prophetic" sees the church through the eyes of the prophet, the "royal" sees through the eyes of the king. The task of the former is to nurture and evoke a critical consciousness of the dominant culture while the latter seeks to preserve it. Brueggemann believes that the church has historically been co-opted; its perception blurred; and the imagination of the people restricted by the climate of affluence, oppressive social policy, and static religion that he believes inevitably accompany the royal imagination. The prophet and the king see the world very differently. Their visions for the future, understanding of possibilities, and choices are a function of their different imaginations. Brueggemann pleads with the church to cultivate a prophetic imagination. In the Old Testament the prophet spoke for God. To speak for God, the prophet had to first listen to God. My hope is that as this book unfolds you will ask, which imagination shapes the governing and management processes of your congregation and other church organizations you are a part of? Is it the imagination rooted in the culture of business or in the passion for listening to God and obeying? This question may not be easy to answer, because the boundaries are not always clearly marked, but it is one that the church must continually ask.

My hope is that you will find in the chapters that follow encouragement to reimagine church governance and management, to envision a model focused first on listening to God. I hope, too, that you will find the practical insights necessary to begin. Still, this is not a how-to book; you will need to discover what works for you and your board as you seek to listen with the gifted people who surround you. Some time ago Loren Mead, Episcopal priest, consultant, and founder of the Alban Institute, authored a small booklet, "The Whole Truth," in which he listed twelve points about church life. The last two are especially important: "You won't get anywhere if you don't start from here," and "Ministry is a journey, not a destination."[4] Leading your board and management structures toward a deeper dependence on listening is indeed a journey. That journey is deceptively easy and incredibly challenging. You never arrive; you simply, like the apostle Paul, press on. But I have never found anyone who, once embarked, would consider any alternative.

1

My Introduction to Church Governance

MY PERSONAL JOURNEY INTO CHURCH GOVERNANCE AND administration began at a Lutheran church in Orange County, California, in 1972. The congregation was a vibrant and growing community filled with hundreds of mobile young families like us from all over the country, who found themselves "neighbors" in the nonstop world of Southern California. While both my wife and I had regularly attended church all our lives, being a part of a congregation that so obviously enjoyed worshiping and working together was a completely new experience. With our three young children in tow, we plunged in, teaching Sunday school, starting a small group ministry, and traveling to Tijuana, Mexico, on mission trips. The congregation soon became the center of our life. Within a short time I was elected to the congregation's governing board. By the time the US Air Force reassigned me to Omaha, Nebraska, three years later, I had served one two-year term and had been elected to another. Like my colleagues, I brought what I learned in my professional career during the day straight into the evening meetings of our governing board. I gave all that I had. A plaque over my desk commemorates those years; the inscription reads, "Articulate Spokesman for Christ, Loving Servant to His Church."

Time has dimmed the names of people and the details of our work, but I remember meetings filled with energy and the feeling that members of the board were truly doing something worthwhile. We met at least twice a month, so the time commitment was significant, especially for those of us who also commuted an hour or more each day to work. We worked hard to offer worship services and educational programs, bring in new members, build community, and minister to the poor, but I don't remember anyone ever asking what God desired. We simply assumed that our collective pursuits aimed at growing our congregation were what God wanted us to be doing, and we did it as best we could.

Each board I have served on or worked with since then has had its own unique culture. Some have been very relational and mission focused like my first board, others very businesslike with little emphasis on relationships. Still others have simply muddled along with no apparent guiding focus or coherent process for making decisions. Some board meetings have routinely been emotionally charged; other boards have chosen to avoid conflict when they meet. Some boards have been powerful; others mere ciphers in a maze of activity. Most meetings offered devotions and an opportunity for at least an opening prayer; some occasionally included elements of worship. A few boards included Bible study, and every now and then a board meeting might include song or a time of silence. Virtually all church-related meetings I have been a part of have been devoted to the business of the institution, often within a well-established polity that further circumscribed what could be done and how. Each board used a type of parliamentary process based on the will of the majority of people present. Some were quite proficient in parliamentary procedure; others simply groped along. Most boards were made up of people who were working in or retired from business or government, felt comfortable with the process of governance and administration, and wanted to serve God. When I had the opportunity to chair governing boards, I tried to do everything as efficiently and effectively as possible. I worked hard to establish a congenial atmosphere, make certain everyone had the best information available, minimize conflict, and keep the process moving following *Robert's Rules of Order*.

In 1999 I entered training to become a spiritual director and was introduced to the contemplative traditions of the church. The contrast between my governing board experience and the prayer and discernment practices I learned in my training to become a spiritual director was stark. Soon after completing my training, I participated in a workshop for pastors and chairpersons of the governing boards of large nondenominational congregations. I had the opportunity to talk about the link I believed existed between historic Christian contemplative practices and contemporary church governance. The response was universally skeptical. To most, the task was to reach "the lost," and they were in the business of developing and offering the experiences necessary to do that; time spent on discernment was time wasted. One pastor shared, with evident pride, that his governing board was made up entirely of successful men who had worked their way up through the world of business. A look around the room told me that most of those present agreed that a governing board made up of successful businessmen was a highly desirable goal.

There was a time when I would have also taken pride in such a collection of successful business talent, but that time had passed. My experiences had led me to believe that the thinking and imagination that enable individuals to succeed in business and government do not necessarily prepare boards for the range of challenges faced by the church, nor do they embrace the voices and values of the people whose personality, talents, and experiences simply do not fit well in governing boards whose primary concern is the business of the church. Yet all people can hear God and know God's desires, and all have been gifted by the Spirit in important ways. Are their gifts and insights not also an important part of discerning the desires of God's heart and carrying them out?

The Institutional Tradition

To better understand contemporary North American church governance, we need to go back through European culture and the early church to ancient Israel. Governance in that world was built on the extensive, highly interconnected, supportive, and well-established network of largely self-sufficient families, clans, and tribal units. Roles were clear, and the expectations of one another remained essentially the same from generation to generation. The ancient Hebrews understood themselves to be the heirs of God's promise to Abraham. Their religious life was central to everything, expectations were well defined, and obedience was expected. Life was linked to the land and its fruits. Behavior and consequence were closely coupled. Leadership came in the form of a few strong individuals, almost always men. Abraham, Joseph, and Moses guided the Hebrews during their wanderings, Joshua during the conquest. Over the next two centuries a series of regional heroes and heroines, whose stories are told in the book of Judges, helped rescue various tribes from local threats. Despite the efforts of the judges, the situation deteriorated. The old Hebrews consistently turned their back on God and followed the ways of the people who surrounded them. The biblical story of this period closes with the observation, "In those days Israel had no king; everyone did as they saw fit" (Judg. 21:25).

The pressure for the Hebrew nation to adopt the governance forms of its more successful neighbors was overwhelming. The people, caught in the chaos of a system of national governance that they believed was no longer working for them, clamored for a more centralized governing structure led by a king. With a king, however, would come a kingdom, and with a kingdom would come an administrative structure to manage the kingdom's affairs that would need to be supported from the people's own pockets. The cost would be significant. There was a slight problem, however: the ancient Hebrews' troubles stemmed from not listening to God, not from their system of government.

From Saul's anointing to the Babylonian exile, the nation's experience with kings and their arch critics, the prophets, dominates the spiritual, military, and political landscape of the biblical narrative. The nation prospers and falls depending on each successive ruler's obedience to God. Each is judged by the standards of Israel's second king, David. Psalm 78:70–72 offers the description of David's leadership; "He chose David *his servant* . . . ; from tending the sheep he brought him to be the shepherd of his people. . . . And David shepherded them with *integrity of heart*; with *skillful hands* he led them" (italics added).

Between the return from exile and the emergence of the early church, Israel was ruled by a succession of governments that ranged in complexity from the simple organization established by Nehemiah to rebuild Jerusalem's walls to the elaborate bureaucracy necessary to support Herod's grand building projects and the cult of religious leaders that surrounded the temple. Politically and militarily, Israel was the "doormat" of the region, continually at the mercy of the nations that surrounded it. The glory days of David and Solomon were long gone. The faithful longed for a king of David's stature and charisma, a Messiah, who would lead them in casting off the chains of oppression, reestablishing the religious practices prescribed in the Torah, and restoring peace and prosperity to the land. Some believed Jesus was this king, but Jesus repeatedly discouraged this connection, stressing that his kingdom was not a kingdom like those set up for military, political, social, or economic purposes that required resources and administration to sustain itself. Jesus's kingdom was one set up to serve, with leaders who were to seek to have the "mind of Christ" (Phil. 2:5 NJB).

Governing issues change in the New Testament. The circumstances shift from a sovereign nation of ethnically homogeneous people rooted in a land given them by God to scattered small communities of increasingly diverse people growing in the teaming urban centers of the Roman Empire. Kings disappear. Unlike Israel, the new church was not encumbered with the material demands of being a public organization; all the political, military, economic, and social issues of state were gone. Gone too was the intimate relationship to the land and the temple where God resided. The principle figures were now elders who oversaw small groups of people meeting together regularly, often in homes. Like the father in a family, the *elder* was responsible for seeing that people in his charge came to know and live their faith. *Deacons* were appointed to carry out acts of service. The principal concern in the early New Testament church was on establishing and maintaining identity, assimilating new people from diverse cultures into its familial life, caring for the needy, and spreading the good news in Jesus.

For more than two hundred years the early church was able to devote the majority of its attention to the spiritual life of the community in the private sphere of the household without having to be overly concerned with the administrative work inherent in developing and maintaining larger organizations. As Christianity grew and began attracting increasing numbers of people from the municipal ruling elites, that situation changed. Many of these new people were schooled in the institutions of public life. As they were assimilated, they shared their experience and expertise. This influx of people who had worked in Roman administration provided the early church with skills necessary to accommodate the growth that soon followed and helped put in place the institutional structures and mindset that have supported and shaped church life since then.

As the need for coordination among congregations in urban centers became apparent, an "elder of elders" or *bishop* role emerged. By the fourth century the church had buildings, established roles, and specific governing structures that needed continuous attention. The adolescent church began to take on the aura of urban government, and a hierarchical structure like that found in the Roman system of administration emerged. The conversion of the Roman emperor, Constantine, ushered in a period of rapid growth in the church, often by the assimilation or conquest of whole populations. The Roman Empire's decline and the unraveling of the fabric of society that began occurring a few centuries later placed greater pressure on the church to offer stability and order through its organizational and administrative structures. As the need for organization increased, the more charismatic leadership witnessed in the early church gave way to the more positional power of the episcopal offices, and the church became more and more like a kingdom.

The history of how the institutional church organized itself in response to various pressures from within and without and the arguments used to support the myriad of organization and leadership structures that developed is long and complicated, and I do not wish to attempt to summarize it. There is no story of success, only a path of experiences from a kingdom that lost its way, to small communities of believers gathered in settings where they were unencumbered by the need to sustain complex organizational structures or to be concerned with the society that surrounded them, to a powerful state-like institution in a fragmented European culture. Our contemporary image of the church and the expectations of governance continue to be influenced by this legacy and the relationships among church, government, and commercial interests that evolved.

The Reformation brought many changes, but it did not fundamentally alter the institutional nature of the Western church. The Reformers were also associated with various political power structures and people of wealth. The numbers of adherents to each reformer conveyed political power, and the development and maintenance of doctrine assured the cohesion necessary for each group to define itself. Each movement within the Reformation led to new hierarchies and often to territorial claims, armed confrontation, and all too often a loss of life. The one major exception is the Society of Friends, founded in seventeenth-century England, where the conviction that each person possessed truth led to a system of governance that discouraged hierarchy and conformance to specific beliefs and emphasized communal discernment and consensus.

As forms of representative government emerged in Europe and later in North America, so did the system of parliamentary law. In the late 1800s the parliamentary model used in the US Congress was adapted by United States Army Brigadier General Henry M. Robert to provide a way of conducting more orderly meetings in churches and other organizations. Since its introduction, *Robert's Rules of Order* has become the primary system for deliberation and decision making in the governing and administrative bodies of US and Canadian churches. *Robert's Rules of Order* is an effective way of systematically collecting input, ensuring majority rule and minority voice, offering widespread participation in decision making, and maintaining openness to critical feedback in a context that presumes conflicting interests. God certainly can and does work through church bodies using *Robert's Rules*, but *Robert's Rules* and the emphasis on the business of the organized church that has been the focal point of much church activity since the time of Israel's kings typically ignore or diminish ways of knowing that extend beyond data and rational thought.

The Contemplative Voice

The early church was born into a culture heavily influenced by a Greek philosophy that favored the life of the mind, contemplation, over involvement in the work necessary to sustain people in the everyday world. Early Christians were continually confronted with the perceived need to choose between a more active life that included overseeing congregations, evangelizing, and caring for the needy as well as commerce and field labor and a more contemplative life of withdrawal to a solitary existence centered in prayer and reflection. By the end of the fourth century some men and women were opting for the latter and had begun to withdraw from their growing faith communities in urban centers to lead lives of self-denial in the wastelands of interior Egypt and desolate spots in Syria and Palestine. Clearly the desire to lead a more contemplative life was an important factor for most, but there is evidence that some people were also rejecting both the administrative culture of the Roman Empire that was creeping into the church and the dilution of the faith that they perceived to be occurring.[1] The early Christians who fled to the desert soon found that they needed the discipline and structure many had spurned. Saint Benedict (AD 480–547) was among the first to attempt to offer it. He authored a set of rules that prized a rhythm of both contemplative practices and work. The value of the rhythm practiced by the Benedictines caught the attention of Pope Gregory the Great, a former monastic, and in AD 596 he sent the Benedictines to evangelize the Anglo-Saxons in what would become Great Britain. In doing so Pope Gregory connected contemplative life to the missional practices of evangelization and care for the poor that the Greeks had philosophically separated.

Over the centuries European monastic communities that developed out of life in the eastern deserts grew in size and land holdings. As they did, they found themselves faced with the need to become efficient administrators and to deal with issues associated with managing property while seeking to maintain their contemplative values. The world outside the monastery walls was also in need of help, and by the thirteenth century many men and women pledged to the monastic values of poverty, chastity, and obedience were living and working directly in the countryside and towns. The contemplative life and the active life were two sides of the same coin, and they were mutually dependent.

A few years ago our son moved to Edinburgh, Scotland. As my wife and I have trekked the Scottish countryside with him to learn more about his new home, we have been drawn to countless church and monastery ruins. Our parallel readings on the history of early Christianity in Great Britain have helped us understand the dynamics that impelled people to move so much stone in so many places to build simple hermitages, monasteries, and great cathedrals. Douglas Dales, chaplain and head of religious studies at Marlborough College, in *Light to the Isle: Missionary Theology in Celtic and Anglo Saxon Briton*, examines the church in Britain up to about AD 800. In his closing remarks, Dales observes that monasticism and mission always flourished and waned together in the early mission to the British Isles. It did little good to build churches and evangelize if the effort was not accompanied by the development of monasteries devoted to prayer and learning. Likewise, monasteries not accompanied by the organization of church and commitment to mission soon failed.

Despite the interdependency of monastic life and mission observed by Dales, many theologians continued to tout the superiority of the contemplative life away from the outside world up to the dawn of the Renaissance. Renaissance thinkers saw the creativity of God in the work of craftsmen and artists. Lee Hardy, professor of philosophical theology at Calvin Theological Seminary, writes, "Thus work, in light of the Renaissance understanding, was no longer something that binds us to the necessity of nature, . . . rather by it we can express our essence as free, creative, and sovereign beings, thereby achieving divine status."[2]

The German monk Martin Luther, generally regarded as the father of the Protestant Reformation, further clarified the importance of work. He rejected the persistent view that one person's work was somehow superior to another's, whether priest or public servant. Luther believed all work that was not self-indulgent consumption or accumulation was a part of God's grand design and that men and women are the hands and feet of God in feeding, nurturing, and healing God's people. In Luther's view, all honorable vocations—be they monk, field hand, domestic servant, or king—are equal in the sight of God. Living out one's vocation was an act of obedience to God instead of something that took attention away from God.

Ignatius of Loyola, a Spanish priest, founder of the Society of Jesus, and a contemporary of Luther's, also believed that life could not be separated as Greek philosophical tradition attempted to do. Ignatius believed that God was continually working in people's lives to encourage them to become more Christlike and to lead them to the place where God is best served and the people are best helped. Each person's responsibility was to listen and respond. Ignatius therefore placed a great deal of emphasis on awareness of our external and internal worlds and on being indifferent to created things and potential outcomes. The spiritual disciplines, which were the staples of contemplative life, were essential to this increased awareness and attitude of indifference. Ignatius also believed both rational thinking and nonrational ways of knowing were essential to true discernment. The voices of Benedict, Luther, and Ignatius resonate across the centuries. Their thoughts and practices loom large in the vision of people seeking a way to govern and administer church organizations that is not enslaved to the business of the institutional church.

North American Business Enterprise

The discussion thus far has highlighted the development of the church as an institution, the contemplative movement, and the values assigned to work. Each of these topics is part of the church's story, but another subject needs to be more fully acknowledged to better understand contemporary church governance in North America. It is business enterprise. Over the past century church governing boards and people working in administrative roles within the church have been increasingly influenced by the culture of North American business enterprise. Many congregations and other church organizations bear the philosophical and operational stamp of business and government employers in their area. I have served on boards dominated by the prevailing perspectives and management practices of local agribusiness, the telephone company, a US Air Force base, aerospace research and manufacturing, and various agencies of the US government. In Sunday school and from the pulpit, clergy and lay leaders of these congregations talk about the relational model of the body of Christ, spiritual gifts, and the servant image of Jesus as theological concepts, but they generally fail to connect them to the boardroom, where prevailing business models reign. Indeed, I would argue, based on my research and experiences, that the impact of business-enterprise thinking not only strongly influences church boards but also extends to the way people think about their life, read the Bible, and practice their faith.

The emphasis on business enterprise in our society has resulted in what Betty Sue Flowers, business consultant, poet, editor, and a professor at the University of Texas, calls the "economic myth." The economic myth is the perception that real value resides in things that can be quantified and measured in economic terms and in images that convey a sense of economic worth. Flowers believes the importance our society attaches to economic value is so strong that it has become the foundational story informing the thinking and behavior in all domains of North American life. Her concern, and mine, is that where economic value becomes the norm, the significance of things that cannot be quantified or described in concrete images, and our capacity to talk about them, may be lost. My experience with church boards suggests, and the reports of participants in my research confirm, that the economic myth is real, and that it combines with the church's institutional legacy and the parliamentary process church boards rely on to create a culture of governance that overemphasizes activities that can be quantified and defined. Where that happens, people whose style and talents are less compatible with the emphasis on business tend to withdraw, and their insights are largely lost.

Considerable evidence exists that governing boards that have emerged from this heritage are not healthy. Why, then, is it important to pay further attention to what goes on in the workplace? Two reasons. First, as already pointed out, what goes on in workplaces day to day affects how people perceive, talk about, and carry out church governance and administration. Second, the emerging interest in spirituality in business, which I will talk about next, offers evidence that the culture of contemporary organizations can integrate spiritual practices such as those lived out in the contemplative traditions and continue to compete in the marketplace.

Business Enterprise and Spirituality

The nature of work has changed dramatically since the sixteenth century; so, too, have individual and societal experiences and expectations of what work is. Physical survival and working within one's social station have given way to a desire for finding meaning and striving for upward mobility. As work across North America has changed, so has the structure of our society. We have transitioned from a society largely comprised of individuals working for themselves in rural settings and small towns to a highly urbanized people working for a wide variety of corporate entities and governmental organizations. The vast majority of people now find themselves spending increasingly long hours working in roles that are but one step in a long process over which they have little control. As a result, work too often dehumanizes rather than enriches the life of the worker. Many speak of this dehumanization as the "loss of soul." The word *spirituality* is typically used in conversations about recovery of the soul in the world of work.

In the past twenty years, restoring the soul in work has become a discernable force in the contemporary North American workplace. Patricia Aburdene, influential futurist and advocate for corporate transformation, observes in her book *Megatrends 2010* that this yearning for the recovery of soul is receiving so much attention in the business community that the emergence of spirituality in the workplace stands as today's greatest megatrend. I have followed this trend since I was first introduced to spirituality in a leadership development program for senior business executives in the early 1990s. Today a growing body of literature in both professional management and academic communities chronicles the growth of spirituality in the corporate world of North America.

The interest in spirituality in the workplace indicates that companies are recognizing that emphasizing the *business* of the organization is not enough. So why do so many church governing boards slavishly follow a model that continues to accentuate business activities and perspective? I believe there are at least five reasons.

- The perception that church governance is primarily centered in the business affairs of the church too often limits participation in governance to those who are interested or feel competent in business activities.
- Too many people simply do not believe they are capable of or responsible for discerning God's will. They understand business; spiritual matters are someone else's responsibility.
- Language and metaphors reinforce the business and organizational culture. Words like *leadership* and *organization* invariably evoke images of hierarchical relationships that may limit a church board's response to more "adaptive work."
- It is difficult to imagine what we have not personally experienced. People use *Robert's Rules* rather than corporate spiritual discernment to make choices simply because they are familiar with the former and not with the latter.
- An unwillingness to develop relationships that can transcend differences and a simple reluctance to submit our corporate lives to God are also reasons why the church preserves the ways we have done business. Simply stated, we understand how the current system works, and we are reluctant to embark on a path that may shift the power dynamics.

The task of each church governing board is to discern God's yearnings and to creatively commit their heart, soul, mind, and strength to that work. To do this work, governing boards must be attentive to what is going on within and around the church. The world's growing interest in spirituality may itself be calling the church to look again at the contemplative practices inherent in spirituality and their contribution to the church's health and effectiveness. Those who study and interpret new social, environmental, economic, and political currents in the contemporary world and the ways in which these currents help or hinder God's creative and redemptive work may offer valuable input for governing boards.

Governing Board Spirituality

In his book *A History of Christian Spirituality*, Urban Holmes III, who was dean of the School of Theology at the University of the South at the time of his death in 1981, examines the spiritual lives of Benedict, Luther, and Ignatius together with a host of other men and women whose diverse voices have shaped the church down through the centuries. *Spirituality* is the term Holmes uses to describe the relationship each had with God. Holmes uses two measures to describe how they (and by extension Christian humanity over time) sought to know the triune God. The first measure Holmes uses is our perception of the nature of God. Is God ineffable, unnameable, and vaster than any known category, or are the qualities and ways of God fully revealed in anthropomorphic imagery and a more literal reading of Scripture? The second measure is how people come to know about God. Do we come to know God through logic and reason or through experience and intuition? Holmes concludes that spiritual health is not rooted in one path or another but in being able to envision God as both mystery and fully revealed through logic and reason as well as experience and intuition.

Corinne Ware, assistant professor of ascetical theology at Seminary of the Southwest, used Holmes's work to develop a tool to assess corporate and individual spirituality. I have used her Spirituality Wheel[3] over the years in conjunction with another much more sophisticated instrument known as the Success Style Profile[4] to help groups of leaders in the Lutheran church understand their collective spirituality and how they receive, process, and act on information. The results from these two instruments reveal a pattern in contemporary church governance that tends to emphasize verbal communication, rational argument, conceptual thought, logical analysis, formulation of vision, goal setting, and preparation of plans. People tend to value what can be quantified and measured in economic terms and images that convey a sense of economic worth. The board culture associated with the above emphases and values tends to use anthropomorphic language and imagery to describe God and to frame conversations about God in intellectual terms. Ware uses the shorthand term *head spirituality* to describe individuals and groups who are drawn to the logic, order, and consistency inherent in this type of spirituality. What is undervalued in the above picture of board life are silence, mystery, feeling, intuition, dialogue, reflection, discernment, a sense of the rhythms of life and the church year, integrating worship and prayer into church governance, and a greater awareness of what is happening in the world outside themselves (perceptual thinking).

To the extent church governing boards exhibit a bias toward head spirituality, they are better equipped to meet challenges where the problem is familiar and solutions usually involve applying the right amount and right type of resources and expertise. This type of board work is what Ron Heifetz calls *technical work*. Heifetz is senior lecturer in public leadership and cofounder of the Center for Public Leadership at Harvard University's John F. Kennedy School of Government. Heifetz says that the culture of thinking that supports technical work, however, is often ill-prepared for challenges that require organizations to figure out what needs to be done and then learn how to do it. Heifetz terms the type of work that requires corporate learning *adaptive work*. Most governing work within the church is technical. This is because most challenges organizations face, such as visioning, goal setting, planning, program development, staffing, acquiring property, and financial management, are technical in nature, but it is also because boards have been conditioned to see their work through the technical lens. If churches could move away from our habitual preoccupation with business we might see that more of what we treat as technical work would be more adaptive work. The problem is we do not typically take time to see the adaptive potential.

The Invitation

When Jesus ascended to heaven, he did not leave behind an organization staffed by people in a variety of designated hierarchical roles, policy manuals, and a succession plan. Jesus left a model of behavior; a community of people whom he called, taught, and shared his life with; and the promise of the presence of the Holy Spirit to all who believe. It is the Spirit who gathers, guides, governs, inspires, equips, sustains, and connects the people who form the body of Christ. It is this same Spirit whom the leadership within the church must seek and follow. Too often we forget that the Holy Spirit founded the church; we abandon discernment and developing relationships because they don't fit neatly into our countless programs, time-compressed agendas, perceptions of order, and desire to be in control.

In the zeal to marshal people for the roles in the organization, congregations typically overlook the possibility that the collection of gifts present might be an expression of God's desires for that community. Too often churches recruit leaders to sustain the institution more than develop the body of Christ. The church is blessed with an amazing array of knowledge, talent, and perspectives to be developed and deployed to meet the full range of challenges inherent in spreading the gospel, caring for the needy, and being stewards of creation. My experience suggests that God has gifted people in far greater ways than the institutional church has the capacity to recognize and develop. The problem is that our continued emphasis on the institution's business often limits who serves in governing roles and what gets talked about in board meetings. That seems to me to be poor stewardship of God's gifts and an unnecessary limit on a world of possibility.

I once watched a slow-motion film of the great Olympic sprinter and Dallas Cowboys' wide receiver Bob Hayes in the one-hundred-meter dash. The intensity in his eyes, the rippling and flexing of his sculpted muscles, and the power evident in each stride demonstrated Hayes's amazingly coordinated body and his total focus on one thing, winning the race. Every part of Hayes's being was involved and working together. If Hayes had ignored developing any part of his body or suffered an injury to any part, however minor, he could not have competed successfully, perhaps not even run. The apostle Paul undoubtedly was familiar with athletes in his own time, and his choice of the body as a metaphor for the church is also especially relevant to us. Yet so many governing boards try to *run* with only a small portion of their potential capacity. If all the church's work is the technical work of administering an organization offering products and services, then perhaps all we need for governance is a group of successful business people. But if the majority of the church's work is more adaptive (and I firmly believe that it is), then our reliance on the business model has the potential to significantly limit how we understand God's desires and how we respond.

In his book *The Purpose Driven Church*, Rick Warren, founding pastor of Saddleback Church in Lake Forest, California, states that where God guides, God provides.[5] Warren's simple observation is not new; it is an essential message of the biblical narrative from the beginning, yet churches continually lose sight of the profound truth in Warren's words. Too often church leaders get caught up in the process of creating and managing organizations, especially those committed to doing good things like spreading the gospel and caring for the needy, as I found in my first board. This may indeed be what God desires, but it may also mask the potential for something more.

The research of Chilean biologists Humberto Maturana and Francisco Varela suggests that people tend to see what their genetic predispositions, experiences, and reflections on those experiences have prepared them to see.[6] If Maturana and Varela's work is valid, then we must ask how our long experience in governing boards that emphasize hierarchy, parliamentary law, and business experiences has conditioned us to understand God, perceive the world, and respond. My point is not to denigrate the benefits of institutional forms that have contributed significantly to the church and society and on which we will continue to depend. I am concerned, however, about the subtle ways institutional forms and the economic myth interact to dominate our thinking and create blind spots due to that domination. Both Stanford University anthropologist E. Richard Sorenson[7] and linguist Helena Norberg-Hodge[8] have documented the capacity of institutional cultures that emphasize rational thought, such as those that prevail in North American business and governments, to overwhelm cultures that rely more on feeling and experience. The thinking processes and spirituality evident in leaders in my own church body that I outlined above bear witness to this usually unintended outcome.

The landscape of the contemporary North American church is dotted with men and women in congregations and other religious organizations who are attempting to expand and deepen the spiritual life of their governing boards. These men and women are seeking to move their boards from a head spirituality, which tends to emphasize technical work, toward a more fully developed spirituality, which is capable of more adaptive work, by integrating spiritual practices from the church's historic contemplative traditions into the fabric of governance. Most emphasize spiritual discernment: listening prayer, liturgy, storytelling, and biblical theological reflection to help people listen more attentively to God and to one another. The bulk of this book is devoted to their experiences and mine and what we have learned along the way.

2

A Vision for Church Governance from the Scriptures

So often I hear the argument from members of church governing boards that they don't have time to practice spiritual disciplines, especially corporate discernment. They believe they can't make room to listen to God together because the financial, facility, program, and personnel issues facing the congregation (or other church organization) take precedence. The business aspects of church life are important, but are they the most important concerns for governing boards? Boards whose members feel they don't have time for anything as open ended as listening to God typically spend most of their quality time together on the day-to-day business of the church and putting out organizational fires.

In their book *First Things First*, Stephen Covey, one the most successful and influential leadership consultants in contemporary North America, and coauthors A. Roger Merrill and Rebecca Merrill offer a simple four-part matrix that arranges the tasks organizations must deal with according to their urgency and importance. The authors report that a typical organization spends about 25 percent of its time on issues that are both urgent and important and 1 percent on issues that are neither. The remaining time is spent on work that is either important and not urgent or urgent but not important. Organizations differ dramatically in the time they devote to these two categories. *High performance* organizations spend between 65 and 80 percent of their time on important but not time-urgent tasks, while others spend 50 to 60 percent of their time on work that appears urgent but is less important.[1] The authors' point is that leadership needs to focus on the important and generally non-time-urgent tasks of assessing circumstances and opportunities and gaining and communicating a clear sense of purpose and direction, rather than reacting to less important routine activities and agendas of others.

Allocating time to the important, non-time-urgent work that these authors advocate is clearly essential for congregations, but there is more. Over the years, I have encountered a number of savvy church governing boards that devote considerable time to assessing circumstances and opportunities as well as gaining and communicating a clear sense of purpose and direction, but many do so without ever engaging in any form of corporate discernment. Are there specific corporate discernment practices that every board should follow? No, but effective church governing boards also need the emotional, relational, and spiritual space that corporate discernment offers so that they can move beyond existing attachments and perspectives and listen together in openness and obedience for God's leadings. The good business practices that Covey, Merrill, and Merrill advocate are steps toward becoming a more high-performing organization, but church governing boards are called to be more than high performing. They are called to listen and obey.

In directing their full attention to listening to God together, the biggest obstacle church governing boards face seems to be an inability to envision and describe a credible alternative that people who value a more business-oriented governing board and people who value a more spiritually oriented board can relate to. The conversations and research that form the foundation of this book suggest that credible alternatives exist. The challenge is to articulate an alternative that speaks to both. In this chapter and the two that follow, I will attempt to do that by offering a set of mutually reinforcing insights from the Bible, science, and experiences in the arena of organizational leadership and contemplative practice that I believe are a viable alternative path that puts first things first.

Any journey into the arena of church governance must begin in the Scriptures, for the Scriptures are our common heritage and the foundation of our life together. The Scriptures tell us who God is, how God is at work in our world, and what God desires of us. They talk at great length about purpose, values, and relationships, but what they say about governance has been a matter of debate. David Bartlett, dean and professor at Yale Divinity School, believes the New Testament offers two contrasting approaches for Christian communities. One is organic and open, the second more formal and hierarchical. In his book *Ministry in the New Testament*, Bartlett suggests that Paul emphasized the more organic and open approach to the church's organization (Rom. 12:4–8; 1 Cor. 12:12–30; Eph. 4:11–16; Col. 2:19) because of the potential he saw in that model for being open to the Spirit's movement, while the authors of the more formal, hierarchical models of the pastoral letters (1 Tim. 3:1–13; 4:13–14; Titus 1:5 16) were more influenced by the need to maintain order. Bartlett concludes that it is not one or the other, but what serves the gospel in a specific context that must be followed.[2]

Over time, as I pointed out in chapter 1, church governing boards appear to have been more influenced by the perceived need to maintain order, and they have consistently opted for a more formal and hierarchical approach. In this chapter I highlight seven themes from the Scriptures that I believe invite the church to look toward the more organic model. Those themes are the following:

We the church are called to be servants.
We are blessed by difference.
We are the image of Christ in our world.
We are uniquely gifted by the Spirit.
We are saved by grace through faith for . . . *good works!*
We need sabbath for rest, renewal, and regeneration.
We are a part of a highly interrelated world.

Together these seven themes offer an image of what church governance should be emphasizing. These themes pull increasingly at my heart as I read, pray, listen to, and trust the Word. My research suggests that they touch the hearts of many others too. I offer these themes to you as a place to begin a conversation about how a church might govern itself in a way that helps members listen both to God and to one another and respond in the most effective way. I am well aware that I have not included any material in this chapter that relates to the different forms of governance most often used within the church. That omission is intentional, and my reasoning is simple. So much has been written over the centuries to support this or that governing structure that there is little I can add. More important, however, the people who participated in this research seem to place less importance on formal, hierarchical structures and more emphasis on what best supports the discipline of listening to God together and fosters an openness to the Spirit's movement.

We the Church Are Called to Be Servants

Genesis 1:26–28 tells us that humanity is created in the image and likeness of the Creator. But what is God's image and likeness? In the opening lesson of his two-year *Crossways* Bible study, Harry Wendt, a Lutheran pastor from Australia and founder of Crossways International, shows eight stylized hats representing eight commonly held images of God.[3] Participants are asked to pick the hat that best describes God. Is God someone who knows everything, a policeman out to catch us in our sins, a chef who provides our daily bread, the supplier of what we believe we need to make life pleasant, the great miracle worker, the king of the universe, the puritan taskmaster whose goal it is to make people conform to specific standards of behavior, or the great healer? After asking participants to consider the options, Wendt reminds us that Jesus wore a hat, but it was a hat made of thorns. Ultimately, he suggests that the most appropriate image of God may be that of the servant washing feet in the opening verses of John 13.

As a child, I was continually surrounded by images and stories of the Bible. Love, kindness, and forgiveness were universal themes, but so was the strength of Samson, the cunning and fighting prowess of David, the riches and wisdom of Solomon, the leadership of Moses, and the power of God unleashed through prophets like Elijah. My early Bible story books show a host of well-dressed, privileged people leading armies, sitting on thrones, calling down the power of God, faithfully praying, teaching, healing, playing with little children, or simply walking about and talking. Servants were simply bit players who waited on the central characters. In many ways, servants were synonymous with slaves, and, in my experience, Christians were neither. Over the years the challenges of leadership roles in the military and business made me quite skeptical of the servant model of leadership and its viability, especially in contemporary organizations.

What I could not grasp intellectuality, however, became a part of me in a visceral way one day on the sidewalk in front of the Church of the Saviour's Festival Center on Columbia Road in Washington, D.C. I remember laying my hands on sculptor Jimilu Mason's new life-size bronze of a contemporary Jesus teaching and looking out across the bustling urban neighborhood that surrounds the center. I said simply, "Lord, I don't understand." Suddenly the paradox of being both a servant and a leader made perfect sense, and ever since, my life has been shaped by the John 13:1–17 passage that inspired Mason.

The disciples struggled with the concept of being both servant and leader throughout Jesus's earthly ministry, so much so that when they gathered for the Last Supper, Jesus repeatedly emphasized the importance of being a servant. In the Luke account of that evening, Jesus says, "The kings of the Gentiles lord it over them; and those who exercise authority over them call themselves Benefactors. But you are not to be like that. Instead, the greatest among you should be like the youngest, and the one who rules like the one who serves. For who is greater, the one who is at the table or the one who serves? Is it not the one who is at the table? *But I am among you as one who serves*" (Luke 22:25–27, italics added).

Brennan Manning, former Franciscan priest and friar whose spiritual journey has touched my life and many others, uses John 13 to illuminate the stark contrast between the servant's walk and the upwardly oriented career path that so many of us spend so much of our lives pursuing. In his book *Reflections for Ragamuffins*, Manning writes,

> The beloved disciple presents a mind-bending image of God . . . and what discipleship is all about. What a scandalous reversal of the world's values! To prefer to be the servant rather than the lord of the household is the path of downward mobility in an upwardly mobile culture. To taunt the idols of prestige, honor, and recognition, . . . and to embrace the servant lifestyle . . . are the attitudes that bear the stamp of authentic discipleship.
>
> The stark realism of John's portrait of Christ leaves no room for romanticized idealism or sloppy sentimentality. Servanthood is not an emotion or mood or feeling; it is a decision to live like Jesus. It has nothing to do with what we feel; it has everything to do with what we do—humble service. To listen obediently to Jesus—'If I, then, the Lord and Master, have washed your feet, you should wash each other's feet'—is to hear the heartbeat of the Rabbi John knew and loved.[4]

In Exodus, a trembling Moses asks God what God's name is, and God responds, "I AM WHO I AM" (Exod. 3:13–14). Eventually I AM is manifest in Jesus. This is the same Jesus who on the evening before his death responds to questions from Thomas and Philip saying, *"Anyone who has seen me has seen the Father"* (John 14:4–9, italics added). The I AM who first spoke to Moses from the burning bush is finally revealed. I AM is not a mighty king, nor a warrior, nor a great priest, nor a prophet. I AM is a servant! The twelve-hundred-year journey of revelation from the burning bush is complete. The God who led Israel through its tumultuous life as a nation, slowly revealing to them along the way how love, holiness, justice, and power weave together, is revealed as the servant Jesus.

The story of God's emergence as a servant is much like that of Leo in Nobel Prize winner Hermann Hesse's great story, *The Journey to the East*. Hesse's Leo inspired Robert Greenleaf, then an AT&T vice president and later founder of the contemporary servant leadership movement, to recognize the servant role's importance in leading contemporary institutions. God has chosen to use the form of a servant to help human beings understand that our life is not about our power or importance. Human beings are but a part of creation, but with a special role—the role of a servant. We are not owners or people of privilege; we are stewards and servants.

We Are Blessed by Difference

You may have long recognized the wonderful diversity of people, but it took me awhile to see that difference was essential to the vitality of an organization. Like other military officers and corporate executives, I was well schooled in the politically correct language and actions of the workplace. But growing up in a small town in Indiana surrounded by people essentially like me, and spending successive careers in the bureaucracies of the US Air Force, the defense industry, and the Lutheran church did not exactly immerse me in difference. Each of these bureaucracies was very good in its own way at fostering a relatively homogenous view of the world. The leaders in each culture spoke of the desire to be open, but they were really open to "new" thinking only from people who already thought like them; people who thought differently caused problems. However, we live in a complex and highly interconnected age, one that requires us to hear the voices of people often quite different from ourselves if we are to address the complicated social, political, and environmental issues we face.

The Bible is relatively silent about the value of difference. Genesis 1; Leviticus 25:1–24; Job 38–41; Psalms 8, 19, 65, 104; Proverbs 30:24–28; Matthew 6:25; and Colossians 1:15–20 all speak of or imply a wonderfully diverse, living, and interconnected creation bound together in the triune God, but the theme of differences among people is more elusive. The clearest teaching about differences among people in the Bible may be in Paul's first letter to the church in Corinth. In chapter 12 of this letter, Paul lauds the rich diversity of gifts given by the Spirit to different people and the importance of each of those gifts to the full functioning of the church. The early chapters of that same letter, however, are quite critical of differences that do not emanate from the Spirit and result in destruction of community, heightened individualism, pride, and denigration of others. The value of difference in the Bible therefore seems to depend upon the presence and work of the Spirit. Where God is the focus, difference is valued; where human desires are selfishly pursued, as in the Tower of Babel narrative (Gen. 11:1–9), difference is viewed as opposition to God.

Acts 2, Romans 12, 1 Corinthians 12, and Ephesians 4 each describe a richly gifted community of believers especially equipped to carry out the "different kinds of service" and "different kinds of working" necessary for the common good (1 Cor. 12:4–6). Together, these passages suggest that the task of governance within the church is to listen to the Spirit's movement, discern God's desires, and create the opportunity for people to identify, develop, and use their diverse giftedness. The practical challenges of such stewardship of difference in an organization are formidable, but they are challenges that are familiar to every parent who has sought to recognize and develop their children's differences.

In 1 Corinthians 1:7 Paul assures the Corinthian community that they do not lack anything in order to do what they are called to do. That same promise is true for us. North American Christians live in a promised land truly flowing with the milk and honey of gifts, talents, and resources. But we lose much of our capacity when we limit the scope of governance to the business of the organization and allow it to be carried out by people who tend to think alike. Giftedness can be too easily lost or undeveloped when we do not recognize and encourage it. People who are not encouraged to pursue their gifts either suppress them or move to a more receptive context.

My recognition of the value of difference in governance came in two steps. The first occurred when I was introduced to *Who Speaks for Wolf*. This book by Paula Underwood, an educator and oral historian of the Iroquois, describes a Native American tribe that moves but forgets to consult with one member of its ecosystem—wolf. The question posed by the story is, who speaks for those not represented when choices are made that affect everyone? The second step came a short time later after I led a workshop in Baltimore, Maryland. I had been invited to talk to a group of African American and Hispanic women from various day-care centers around the city about perceptions. To help illustrate the differing ways people perceive the world, learn and remember, make choices, and act upon them, I used the Success Style Profile instrument mentioned in chapter 1. Years of experience using this inventory with people in leadership positions in my national church body and the business community had revealed a closely shared pattern of thinking among business and church leaders. As I viewed the profiles of the day-care providers and talked with them, I was struck by how different their pattern of thinking was from the leadership of our church. The women in this group did not learn and remember, make choices, or act upon them like the leaders of my denomination or the leaders of the government and business institutions that shaped much of the world in which these women lived.

As I made the ninety-minute drive back to my home in southern Maryland, I found myself plagued by questions. Who in my national church body speaks for the women I met today? How are their insights incorporated into the policies and theology that shape my denomination? Who hears their discernments? Who else is not represented in our national church governing processes and the way we think about God? What is lost in understanding God's invitation and the perception of what needs to be done when part of the body is missing? How does their absence affect the church's discernment of the Spirit's call and the development of the giftedness of the people who worship in its congregations? What if four of every five words on this page were redacted, what message would the remaining words convey? The tragedy is that church governing boards systematically exclude many from the process of thinking about God and discerning God's invitation.

We Are the Image of Christ in Our World

If Christians are called to be servants and yet we are different from one another, what is the image we project to the world? The apostle Paul assures the members of the fledgling church in Corinth, in 1 Corinthians 12:27, "You are the body of Christ, and each one of you is a part of it." By extension, we Christians today too are the body of Christ wherever two or three come together. If the church in all its forms is the body of Christ, what does that body tell people about the Christ? Does that body more closely reflect the Jesus of the Gospels or the institutional structures and values of Western culture?

In Romans 12, 1 Corinthians 12, and Ephesians 4, Paul paints a vivid picture of the community of believers. The community of believers is not a kingdom, a corporation, a tribe, or even a family, although it may manifest some aspects of each at various times in various places. The community of believers is a body, a fully integrated, living unity. Ephesians 4:15 and Colossians 2:19 place Christ at the head of this body in a role similar to that of the brain and the associated neural systems of our physical bodies. The body imagery is compelling because it is organic, inclusive, interconnected, interdependent, continually communicating with all its parts and the surrounding environment, and capable of learning and creating. Equally compelling to me are the long sections on love that follow the passages about the church as the body of Christ in 1 Corinthians and Romans and growing into Christ in Ephesians 4. The church reads these passages on the body of Christ over and over in our Sunday services and educational programs, and we regularly hold spiritual gifts classes to help people identify their gifts. Yet when it comes to discerning God's desires and shaping our organizations, we often pay little attention to the incredibly wide range of gifts present and their development for anything other than filling roles within the confines of existing organization structures.

The responses from participants in my dissertation research suggest that North American church organizations do not typically reflect the qualities of the body I have just talked about. Perhaps the gap between theory and practice is simply too great and our imagination too constrained. How might organizations, especially church governing bodies, look and act if they truly believed that people are different, interdependent and connected, gifted by the Spirit, and drawn together as a living body under Jesus to "do good works, which God prepared in advance for us to do" (Eph. 2:10)? What might those governing bodies be like if each person—regardless of the skin color, education, gender, sexual preference, or ethnicity—was valued and his or her gifts accepted as a gift from God? How might we choose to organize if our goal is to develop and employ the rich collection gifts, talents, passions, dreams, personalities, resources, and potential these people bring? What type of leadership is required to be an effective steward of such divine generosity? Indeed, what might a congregation be like if it structured itself around listening to God and stewarding the gifts present today, instead of what sustains the organization and its existing bureaucratic structures?

One would be naive to believe that the church could exist in our world apart from an outward institutional life, just as a Christian cannot have an inner spiritual life apart from an outward bodily life. The church is a myriad of communities of identifiable people with specific names and addresses who live in the world, sometimes prominently and sometimes anonymously, in ways that enhance or detract from the image of a servant Christ. The church includes buildings, properties, public ceremonies, ministries, and leaders with titles and identities. In its various forms, the church is spoken of in the media, recognized for its public efforts on behalf of others, and praised or maligned for its policies on moral issues. Over the millennia since the church's founding, the institutional model has guided most governing boards. The challenge for every congregation and church organization is to see beyond the familiar images and language of the organizational culture in which they live. The church is called to a higher ideal, and I believe the body of Christ is the ideal Scripture establishes for us.

We Are Uniquely Gifted by the Spirit

Acts 2:3–4, 17–18 and 1 Corinthians 12:7, 11 assure us that gifts of the Holy Spirit are given to all believers, regardless of gender, race, ethnicity, social status, or other's perceptions of spiritual maturity, for developing the whole church body. Since the church is an interdependent community and dependent upon the Spirit for everything, it is imperative that our first priority be to discern where the Spirit is moving and then align our thoughts and actions accordingly.

References to the Spirit bracket the biblical narrative. The Spirit of God hovers over the chaotic face of the primordial waters in Genesis 1:2. In Revelation 22:17, the Spirit and the church ("the bride") invite the Christ to "Come!" and urge all who to wish to drink of the "water of life" to come. Between these two stories, God's character, work, and desires are progressively revealed, culminating in the life, work, death, and resurrection of Jesus the Christ and the gift of the Holy Spirit to all believers. The Spirit empowers the community of believers, the church, to continue Christ's work in the world. The Spirit stimulates creativity, motivates leaders, imparts wisdom, invites us to know

God's heart, urges us to seek to be holy, and inspires people to works of service to others and to our world.

The Spirit is not owned or controlled by anyone or any institution, nor is the Spirit limited by what people think or say. The Spirit is continuously present throughout creation and is manifest in the joy, peace, patience, goodness, faithfulness, gentleness, and self-control of the people of God. The Spirit is unity, a unity that transcends the perceptions of harmony and accord among believers. The Spirit is the undivided life force of all of creation, just as Christ is not divided. Since the Spirit is the source of life, hindering the Spirit's movement and work or closing oneself off from the Spirit essentially closes one off from God.

If God is love, as 1 John 4:16 states, then the Holy Spirit must also be love. The goal of each community within the church must be to continually seek to discover what it means for them to love as God loves and to live together in such a way that they and others might better know the God the Bible describes as love (1 John 4:16), spirit (John 4:24), light (1 John 1:5), and a consuming fire (Heb. 12:29). To do this we must listen to and follow the often still, small voice of the Spirit, from inside ourselves and from the world around us, as it competes against all the other voices clamoring for our attention.

We Are Saved by Grace through Faith for . . . *Good Works*!

The writer of Ephesians reminds the church that being saved by grace through faith is just the beginning of being a follower of Christ; we also have *work* to do. "For it is by grace you have been saved, through faith—and this not from yourselves, it is the gift of God—not by works, so that no one can boast. *For we are God's handiwork, created in Christ Jesus to do good works, which God prepared in advance for us to do*" (Eph. 2:8–10, italics added). What is it that believers are supposed to do? Jesus is quite clear in the Gospel of Mark. When asked what the greatest commandment is, Jesus responds, "The most important one . . . is this: 'Hear, O Israel, the Lord our God, the Lord is one. Love the Lord your God with all your heart and with all your soul and with all your mind and with all your strength.' The second is this: 'Love your neighbor as yourself.' There is no commandment greater than these" (Mark 12:29–31).

What is the love Jesus is referring to? How might people know it? What model should we use to live such love into being? What standards should we aspire to? Jesus taught us: "My command is this: Love each other as I have loved you. Greater love has no one than this: to lay down one's life for one's friends" (John 15:12–13), and in Matthew 5:44: "But I tell you, love your enemies and pray for those who persecute you." Yet the work for human beings extends beyond loving God and loving neighbor as themselves; it extends to loving and caring for the whole of creation. Indeed, God's very first words to humans (Gen. 1:26–31) are about their relationship to creation. Some have argued that the natural world exists for the sake of humankind, citing Genesis 1:28 and the words "subdue" in the New International Version or "dominion" in the King James Version to justify their claim. This interpretation seems dramatically counter to the servanthood of Jesus in whose image human beings are created. If God loves the world so much "that he gave his one and only Son" (John 3:16), would God exploit or encourage others to exploit something so dear? Our charge goes beyond simply not exploiting; we are asked to join God in the continuing process of creation. The parable of the talents in Matthew 25:14–27 illustrates this point. The first two servants are rewarded for developing the property that had been entrusted to their care; the third is cast out, not because he squandered the man's property but because *he simply hid it and did not seek to improve it.*

Genesis 1 teaches that creation is good and that humans are created in God's image and given the responsibility to care for creation. Thousands of years ago, before our booming world population and the no-holds-barred pursuit of wealth, God spoke through the law and the prophets to emphasize that as people created in God's image, we are responsible for the care and development of creation. God called us to be kind to the earth, to live within its rhythms, and to make provision for those who for one reason or another fall behind. The laws specify a pace of life that revolves around regular periods of work and rest. They contain stipulations against fouling the places where we live and about caring for our neighbors. They encourage free enterprise, but with a moral center and creation consciousness.

The biblical text makes it clear that the land, the air, the water are God's. Our "ownership" of resources does not include the freedom to exploit; it carries a special responsibility to care for them. The first chapter of Genesis; Leviticus 25:1–24; Job 38–41; Psalms 8; 19; 65; 104; Proverbs 30:24–28; Matthew 6:25; 25:14–30; and Colossians 1:15–20 all assert or imply that the wonderfully diverse, living, and interconnected creation is "owned" by God and bound together in Christ.

Psalm 24:1 affirms the creation narrative. "The earth is the Lord's and all that is in it, the world, and those who live in it." People are stewards, not owners. Christians all over the world and across time have struggled to understand and have debated about the nature of the world. Is the world something to be shunned, as ancient Gnostics suggested, or is it all there is, as naturalists believe? Today all of us can see much more readily the extent of our interconnectedness with creation and the ecological and social disaster that results from the wholesale pursuit of unsustainable lifestyles without regard for their impact on our world. We are not separate from the physical world; we are an integral part of it. The Bible attests that the world is loved by God. The familiar words of John 3:16 are among the first we learn: "For God so loved the world that he gave his one and only Son, that whoever believes in him shall not perish but have eternal life." Caring for creation, and by extension the needy, does not alter God's call to go and make disciples. Both are required. Gathering, developing, and focusing the Spirit's gifts, energies, and resources to carry out these tasks must be a primary concern of each church governing board.

One final comment is necessary. Too often we Christians confine our definition of good works to practicing personal piety, carrying out evangelism, exercising allegiance to the institutional church, and helping the poor. These actions are all important, but they are inadequate, because they are typically understood as personal and do not address the actions of organizations. The world is shaped by countless corporations and other institutions whose enormous power and influence in society goes largely unaddressed in church governing structures and by many Christians. We need to be concerned with the spiritual health of corporations, how people are treated, how corporations use the often vast resources under their control and influence. Robert Greenleaf first awakened me to the importance of corporations' spiritual health when I read his thoughts on the role of large institutions in our society in his book *Servant Leadership: A Journey into the Nature of Legitimate Power and Greatness.* Greenleaf points out that large institutions now carry much of the burden of caring for people that was once largely personal. Those institutions are not always competent; they may even be corrupt. He argues that institutions also need to become servants, and that the church has a major role to play in that work.[5] Several shelves in my library hold stories of companies who make stewardship and spiritual health priorities, and I have listened to a number of senior corporate leaders and consultants talk about their experiences in this area. In their book *A Spiritual Audit of Corporate America: A Hard Look at Spirituality, Religion, and Values in the Workplace,* business consultants Ian Mitroff and Elizabeth Denton offer a glimpse of the range of corporate approaches to spirituality in the United States today. The story of each company they studied is unique. Some have sought to follow a more conservative Christian model; some have been more motivated by social and environmental concerns. Some started with a keen sense of spiritual values, while others endured a great deal of organizational pain before recognizing that their spiritual health was essential to their continued viability. There is no one best model for corporations to follow and there are numerous pitfalls along the way, but that does not mean the church should not try to help corporations become more spirituality healthy and more likely to become good stewards of the tremendous power and influence they are capable of asserting in our world.

We Need Sabbath for Rest, Renewal, and Regeneration

I began this chapter by talking about the challenges so many church governing boards face: never having enough time to take care of business. Perhaps the reason members of boards never have enough time is that individuals do not allow themselves time to regularly step back from their daily activities to rest, to gain a new perspective, and to focus on listening to God. We church members are both the victims and the perpetuators of the myth that long hours on the job and incessant activity are the norm, and we carry those expectations from our work life to the church boardroom and into the other arenas of church life. Genesis 2:2–3 tells us, "By the seventh day God had finished the work he had been doing; so on the seventh day he rested from all his work. Then God blessed the seventh day and made it holy, because on it he rested from all the work of creating that he had done." Remembering the sabbath and keeping it holy became the fourth commandment (Exod. 20:8). Leviticus 25 extends the sabbath to the economic life of the community. This section of the law specifies that every seventh year is to be a sabbath year during which no crops should be planted, and it designates every fiftieth year a jubilee year during which the land should lay fallow, debts should be cancelled, and any property that was sold should be redeemed. While there are questions about both the origin of Leviticus 25's requirements and whether they were ever practiced, the redress of social and environmental imbalances the chapter addresses is certainly in harmony with the prophets' continuing cry for justice and righteousness.

Despite abundant evidence that regular rest, regeneration, and renewal is a critical part of God's pattern, we typically ignore the idea of sabbath in our personal lives and more so in our governing boards. My conversations with governing board members suggest that many like me grew up thinking the fourth commandment was essentially about going to church on Sunday and that the Genesis 2:2–3 account of God resting signaled the end of God's creative activity—all that would ever exist had been created. The vast majority of governing board members I talk with have never heard of Leviticus 25, and when I point it out, they typically reject it without further thought. The significance of sabbath rest, regeneration, and renewal seems to elude many of us as we allow more and more of our lives to be driven by the economic myth I talked about in chapter 1.

Sabbath requirements are a part of the law that provided the spiritually infant Hebrews with guidelines about what it meant to children of a holy, loving, and just God. In the law, God put in place a system to be administered by just people for the benefit of all. These laws covered both personal life and communal life. Ultimately, they were to provide the means for creating a community of peace and prosperity that others would view with admiration and ask, Who is this nation's God, and how might we come to know this God? (Deut. 4:5–8 paraphrase).

The great Christian spiritual traditions all speak of the importance of a sabbath rest and stillness in their disciplines. But taking a regular break from our daily activities to listen to God and to allow those around us to rest and creation to regenerate does not come easily, certainly not for me. I am—in the words of publisher, businessman, and community organizer Gregory F. A. Pierce—"piety impaired."[6] Like many people, I have had difficulty breaking from the frenetic routines that I once allowed to govern my life. In addition, many of us are also "functional atheists," in the words of Parker Palmer, Quaker educator and philosopher; that is, people who believe that ultimate responsibility for everything rests with us.[7] Somehow we seem to fear that life will not go on without us. Here and there, depending on the denomination or church tradition, clergy, academics, and educators are encouraged to take regular breaks from their routines called sabbaticals (the term derives from the Hebrew *sabbath*). Sabbaticals are great for the people fortunate enough to have them, but they are not the same as regularly ceasing activity and stepping aside to rest and encouraging those around us to do the same.

Over time the Jewish people apparently lost sight of the intent of sabbath and began to focus on a vast array of mostly unwritten rules about what constituted acceptable sabbath activity. While many of these rules were undoubtedly helpful to people seeking to live within the true meaning of sabbath, the Gospels suggest that the rules had become burdensome by Jesus's time. Jesus challenged that commonly held view and sought to restore the perspective that sabbath was intended to help people, not discourage them from helping others or receiving help. In Mark 2:27–28 Jesus says, "The Sabbath was made for man, not man for the Sabbath. So the Son of Man is Lord even of the Sabbath." Jesus wasn't saying, "You shouldn't have any rules for the Sabbath." His point was, "The rules must be subject to the higher commandments—to love your neighbor and God."

The ideas of ceasing work and being still for one day each week, regularly correcting the economic imbalances that inevitably occur in the free exercise of commerce, and providing regular rest for the fields and animals that generate wealth seem a bit idealistic and impractical to most of us. History is filled with the bones of prophets and apostles whose words about sabbath rest and redressing economic imbalance have fallen to the ground unheeded. Jesus, too, was ultimately hung on a cross by people who had no intention of relinquishing their privileges for a system of governance grounded in love and obedience to God and led by a servant who would challenge their position of privilege in society. But the call of Jesus to come and follow means we have no option but to work toward a system of governance within the church and beyond that encourages us to live within sabbath rhythms with all our heart, soul, strength, and mind.

We Are a Part of a Highly Interrelated World

The images people have of how the world works inform their perceptions of God and influence their behaviors in organizations. In Genesis 1 the creation process begins with God bringing order to a cosmos that was a "formless void" (Gen. 1:2 NRSV). At the end of the sixth day, "God saw everything that he had made, and indeed, it was very good" (Gen. 1:31 NRSV). But what is the order that God brought out of chaos and declared "very good"? How does it work? Stating it more directly, what does the created order have to do with church governance?

Since the beginning of human history, people have sought to understand how the world they live in works. The motivation for seeking such understanding is simple: when we live in harmony with nature, we are more likely to prosper than when we do not. Ancient observers recognized this relationship as they traced and predicted the movement of heavenly bodies and noted the rhythms in nature. Scientists, naturalists, and theologians continue the quest, devoting enormous resources to understanding the world and how we can make it work for us. Many believe the created world also tells us about the creator. Some rank the book of nature with the Scriptures in importance while others see no connection. I do not intend to enter that debate. What I know is that my experiences in nature and my studies of science have greatly enriched my reading of the Scriptures, my prayer life, and my understanding of God and myself. I affirm what Paul writes in Romans 1:20: "For since the creation of the world God's invisible qualities—his eternal power and divine nature—have been clearly seen, being understood from what has been made, so that people are without excuse."

For most of my life in the church, *order* was the word used to emphasize the need to regulate what could and could not go on in worship services and to rationalize various limitations on what women could and could not do. A "well-ordered" board was one that efficiently deliberated on issues and made timely, well-informed decisions. My own perception of order was informed by theories and observations of classical science that informed my education and work experience. Classical science believed that creation was essentially an elegant machine that had been set in motion by the creator. Often referred to as Newtonian science after the great seventeenth-century English physicist and mathematician Isaac Newton, classical science believed creation was essentially a machine made up of discrete parts that could be understood and outcomes accurately predicted. Contemporary organizations with "org charts" built from pyramids of boxes and lines of authority reflect this view of the world.

In the early 1990s, while participating in a leadership development program for senior executives in the business world, I was introduced to business consultant Margaret Wheatley's *Leadership and the New Science: Learning about Organization from an Orderly Universe*. Most of us in the program were grounded in classical science. We knew little about the "new sciences." Wheatley talked about how they might relate to leadership in our organizations. She argued that our world was not the elegant machine Newton described; instead, everything was interrelated and interdependent, filled with essential information, and far less knowable and predictable than classical scientists ever imagined. Creation could not be taken apart and studied, because as soon as someone tried, the essential character was altered. According to the new sciences, specifically quantum physics, chaos theory, and studies of the brain, our world is an indivisible whole where each part has a unique identity and an important role to play. The world science is describing today sounds a great deal like the organic image of the body Paul uses in Romans 12:4–8; 1 Corinthians 12:12–30; Ephesians 4:11–16; and Colossians 2:19 to describe the church.

When I encountered Wheatley's book, I was in the midst of what turned out to be a twenty-four-year discipline of reading the Bible cover to cover every year in preparation for a series of classes on the Bible that I led. As I reengaged the Scriptures with my fledgling insights from science, familiar passages dealing with creation, abundance and famine, the Spirit's free movement, miracles, the power of natural forces, and the beautiful accounts of nature's wonders took on a deeper meaning. The biblical writers dealt with what could be seen, and they used the language of nature and the images from the everyday world to describe the power and artistry of God. We can relate to the mountains, nighttime skies, deserts, clouds, lakes and rivers, sunrises and sunsets. They are knowable phenomena. But there is another universe we cannot see without the aid of sophisticated research facilities; it is the universe inside the tiny atoms that are the basic building blocks of creation. The subatomic world is a strange world, unlike the creation we experience in everyday life. It is as vast and complex in its smallness as the heavens are in their expanse. It is a world of probabilities and changing identities that defies objective observation. Chapter 3 will focus on this world and the insights it holds for human organizational life.

Is knowing what the subatomic world is like important for church governance? While understanding how the creation works is not essential for salvation, it is essential, I believe, that people who are responsible for church governance recognize that there is far more to the way creation works than most of us who have been focused on the business of the church have been prepared to see. The subatomic world tells us that this is an interdependent world, connected in ways both seen and unseen. Boards who view their organizations as independent and autonomous entities risk misidentifying their work and missing important opportunities to carry out the stewardship of creation and the task of being the body of Christ in the world.

Concluding Thoughts

I believe many people in the church would welcome the opportunity to enter into a dialogue about how church governance might look if we focused on the seven themes listed above. Personally, I find the prospect of beginning such a conversation exhilarating, but the challenges of attempting to change church governance, as many of you know from experience, are formidable. My dissertation research underscores the difficulty church organizations face in seeking to change the way they govern themselves. There were a few notable successes stories, such the effort by the Uniting Church of Australia to make corporate discernment the foundation of their governing process.[8] More often, however, people spoke of failed efforts, discouraged participants, and the lingering consequences of the vigorous debates (some would say fights) over what needed to be done and how to do it.

Moving an organization toward an embodiment of the themes listed above is challenging, because the themes run counter to the way most contemporary organizations work. Because of that, a different approach to introducing them is necessary. The approach needs to be more organic and to come from within; it cannot be imposed. I will spend more time on this subject in later chapters. For now I suggest simply pausing to look at Deuteronomy 6:4–9. This passage has long been one of my favorites. It speaks to the absolute centrality of God, a truth conveyed in God's commandment to love God with our whole being and to carry that love in our heart and our work wherever we go. Perhaps that is why I return to those verses here. We don't need to worry about change yet; that will come. We simply need to begin to make these seven themes the topic of our everyday conversations so that we "talk about them when you sit at home and when you walk along the road, when you lie down and when you get up," and at least symbolically, "Tie them as symbols on your hands and bind them on your foreheads. Write them on the doorframes of your houses and on your gates." My wise friend and mentor Charles Tollett often challenges groups he consults with to ask, "In what ways might we . . ." If the themes I have listed seem like desirable goals, then we need to ask ourselves, "In what ways might we incorporate them into our personal life and the life of our governing boards?" Asking a nonthreatening question such as, "In what ways might we . . ." opens us to the Spirit's wisdom and creates the opportunity for people to share their insights in a spirit of learning versus deciding. I will talk a great deal more about the practical aspects of change in governing boards in later chapters. My purpose here is simply to invite you to consider these seven themes as essential perspectives in helping church governing boards shift their emphasis from the business of the church to listening to God.

3

Insights for Church Governance from the Book of Nature

MANY EARLY SCIENTISTS LIKE NICOLAUS COPERNICUS, Galileo Galilei, and Isaac Newton believed that God had authored two books, the Book of Scripture and the Book of Nature, and that both needed to be read. They believed there could be no contradictions, because both books had the same author. I share that belief. That same reasoning suggests that if the two books do not appear to agree, then we must not yet fully understand them. Historically, our reading of the Book of Nature has focused on the everyday world we can see and feel. This meant that for centuries the "canon" of the Book of Nature was essentially closed. We had no idea about the physical world that lies beyond our everyday experience. Images and experiences that everyone could relate to found a place in the theologies that evolved. By the late nineteenth century some scientists and philosophers arrogantly asserted that *science* was on the verge of revealing virtually everything there was to know about how nature worked. But the twentieth century changed all that as science began exploring the universe beyond our solar system and peeking into the world inside the atom. These revelations plus a pantheon of other important discoveries, such as those in the neurosciences and molecular biology, tell us that the world in which we live is far more extensive and complex than earlier readers of the Book of Nature could have ever imagined.

To attempt to do justice to what the Book of Nature has to say about our relationships, our work, and ourselves would require far more space than a single chapter and a much greater breadth and depth of technical expertise and understanding of the nexus of science and philosophy than I have. My plan, therefore, is to limit my comments to two of the areas most important in my life: the natural world of woodlands, waterways, and farms that I came to love in my childhood and the scientific discipline of physics. My reasoning for selecting these two, apart from the role they play in my life, is simple. The natural world is something each of us can relate to. We can see, touch, hear, and smell it; it's a familiar world where things come in sizes we can relate to and time is something we can measure. Physics, on the other hand, is concerned with the basic structure of the universe and why it works the way it appears to. Physicists regularly deal with sizes and concepts of time that have no counterpart in our day-to-day world and are often difficult for the average person to imagine. All the other sciences (for example, chemistry, molecular biology, cellular biology, neuroscience, psychology, anthropology, economics, sociology) are built on the foundations of the mechanics of matter and energy described by physics. Together, the natural world and physics bracket the key revelations of the Book of Nature.

Prior to encountering Margaret Wheatley's book *Leadership and the New Science* that I mentioned in the preceding chapter, I had never thought of nature as a resource for governing boards. The forests, streams, and farms I loved as a boy growing up in rural southeastern Indiana had been pushed to the margins of my life during my successive careers in the US Air Force, defense industry, and the church. I was focused on the standard fare of organizational life: getting things done in the here and now and being successful. The science I was most familiar with was the science the Air Force relied on to develop the technologies necessary to build and operate aircraft, ballistic missiles, and satellites. That science viewed the natural world primarily as the source of the raw materials needed to build weapon systems and the environment in which we operated them. My church experience added little. Bible studies and sermons seemed to look at creation in highly simplistic and anthropomorphic ways that emphasized nature's beauty or attempted to refute evolution on the basis of theology. My own "Book of Nature" was essentially frozen in the practical everyday world of people working in hierarchical organizations to develop and build more and better things to improve our lives and to save souls.

My reintroduction to the wonder and excitement of the natural world I had known as a youth coincided with my early experiences in servant leadership, exposure to spirituality in corporations, and introduction to Christian spiritual practices. These four themes have remained tightly woven ever since. It would be impossible, therefore, for me to talk about governance without including each of them. Together they shape my imagination of what church governing boards can become. I have not been alone; revelations about the natural world that have emerged in the past century have also drawn the interest and stirred the imagination of many others scattered about the church. The appropriateness of the revelations about the natural world to church governance is further demonstrated by the many books on organizational leadership being written for the business world that integrate learnings from science with the philosophy and practice of leadership and governance, and the popularity of those books among church leaders.[1] Finally, God's first recorded words to human beings in Genesis 1 are about caring for and developing creation. The biblical narrative introduces the necessity of regular sabbath rest, a system of laws regulating human behavior in accordance with God's plan, and the repeated reminder that all of creation, including humanity, belongs to God and that creation is holy. Human beings are stewards of creation. The Bible tells us how we are to live within creation; it does not tell us how creation works. Our stewardship requires us to understand how God's creation works and to live within those parameters. To do that, we must rely increasingly on science.

The World of Science

Before talking more about the Book of Nature and church governance, I need to offer a few perspectives on science. My experience suggests that too many people in governing roles within the church view science with a palpable level of mistrust and misunderstanding. They do not see it as a source of either theoretical or practical insight for governance. Too often science and religion are cast as opponents in a contest for human attention and allegiance; such ought not to be the case. Science is concerned with understanding the natural world; it is a disciplined process of rational inquiry into how our world works in much the same way that theology is the rational inquiry into the Scriptures. Science shares a common language that extends across cultural, linguistic, and national boundaries in a way that allows scientists everywhere to continually develop and exchange knowledge about what they are learning. Scientists are a highly diverse community of people engaged in a wide variety of professional pursuits who are intensely loyal to their field of inquiry and committed to probing the "secrets" of the world and making their results known. The discipline science brings to the exploration of the natural world, the proliferation of perspectives and investigations, and the challenge of continued peer review helps science develop and maintain an extraordinary level of information and intellectual integrity.

Contemporary science embraces many disciplines. Arthur Peacocke, a biochemist, former dean of Clare College at Cambridge University, Anglican priest, and winner of the Templeton Prize for his contribution to the understanding of science and religion, offers a table in his book *Theology for a Scientific Age: Being and Becoming— Natural, Divine, and* Human.[2] The table provides a hierarchy of scientific inquiry in ascending order of complexity, from physics to the study of human culture. Peacocke's Level 1 begins with physics, but includes other sciences such as chemistry, geology, and astrophysics that build on the physical structures defined in physics. Level 2 includes the myriad of scientific disciplines that deal with biological systems such as cellular biology, anatomy, physiology, botany, zoology, and ecology. The neurosciences are included in Level 2 but separated because of the brain's unique role in life and its complexity. Level 3 includes those sciences that study the behavior of living organisms such as cognitive, developmental, comparative, and ecological psychology. Level 4 includes fields of scientific inquiry that focus on behavior across societies such as linguistics, economics, sociology, and anthropology.

Science presupposes an intelligible universe, one that can be known to humanity if we will devote the time and resources necessary to probe it. Albert Einstein, often viewed as the father of modern science, is reported to have observed that the only incomprehensible thing about the universe is its comprehensibility.[3] In his book *Science and the Trinity: The Christian Encounter with Reality*, John Polkinghorne, who distinguished himself in the field of elementary particle physics before becoming an Anglican priest and president of Queens' College Cambridge, states that science allows us "to understand regimes that are remote from everyday experience and whose character demands highly counterintuitive ways of thinking if we are to properly comprehend them."[4] According to Polkinghorne, our capacity to understand the universe rests on two remarkable qualities. The first is the way the natural world at its most basic level—the level studied by physicists—opens itself to mathematical description. The second is our human ability to think mathematically and to develop equations that allow us to accurately describe what nature appears to be doing and to explore what we cannot yet test for.[5]

Early science included both observing life and interpreting the meaning of what was being observed. Contemporary science generally seeks to divorce observation and meaning. Science's goal in attempting this separation is unbiased objectivity. In real life, of course, such objectivity is unattainable, science like all other human endeavors is filled with assumptions and judgments, but the quest for objectivity continues. As science bores into creation, it slowly removes mystery and replaces it with knowledge; but with each new step, new questions and new mysteries continually emerge. Science is not capable of providing all the answers to questions about how the world works or why it works the way it does, but science does offer a continuing stream of insight into the wonders of creation. The church needs to pay more attention to these insights if it is to more fully imagine and attempt to realize the potential in its role as steward of creation and the gospel. Peacocke writes, "The multiple and diverse pictures and features of the natural world . . . are of immense significance for our understanding the content of its structures, entities, and processes, and needless to say, of immense significance also for human beings in interpreting their world."[6]

The History of Science

The history of science is long and complex. The story is generally told in terms of major discoveries that changed our understanding of the world, such as the mechanics of our solar system revealed by Nicolaus Copernicus, Galileo Galilei, Isaac Newton, and Albert Einstein[7] and the mechanics of the world inside the atom first hypothesized by physicists such as Niels Bohr, Paul Dirac, Albert Einstein, Werner Heisenberg, Max Planck, and Erwin Schrodinger.[8] But the general movement of science is a slow, steady, often fragmented exploration, replete with failures and false starts across an increasingly broad spectrum of specialties. Scientific exploration is spurred on by the highest ideals—the desire to know and the quest to meet human needs; it also depends on the very practical realities of money and the technology necessary to observe various phenomena.

Isaac Newton has a unique place in this historical narrative because of the importance of his contribution to science and mathematics and because his name is often used (unfairly) in contemporary literature to denote an archaic approach to leadership and governance. Newton's contributions, like those of Einstein, changed the trajectory of science. His understanding of motion and gravity and his development of calculus are monumental accomplishments. The publication of his *Philosophia Naturalis Principia Mathematica* (1687) marks the birth of classical physics.[9] In the centuries following its publication, many others such as John Dalton, Michael Faraday, and James Clerk Maxwell made major contributions to the growing body of scientific knowledge.[10] Together these early scientists provided the foundation for the rapid advances in science and technology that have characterized the last few centuries in the Western world. Classical physics fostered the belief that the world could be observed, deconstructed, mathematically described, and ordered and outcomes predicted. This belief soon permeated the organizations being created across society and contributed to the leadership and organizational models that folks like me brought to the arena of church governance.

While classical physics was an important step in understanding our world and is still heavily relied on, it has proven to be incomplete. The dawn of the twentieth century brought new theories about the nature of light, the character and extent of outer space, the elasticity of time, the indeterminate world inside the atom, and the capacity of large complex natural systems (such as weather) to order themselves. These discoveries have forced people today to recognize that nature is far more than classical science ever imagined, and they invite us to reexamine what the natural world has to say about how we envision organized human activity. But old ways of thinking resist change, especially when they are deeply embedded in the structures and roles people rely on for order in their everyday lives. The historical importance of hierarchy, control, and predictability in organizations combined with classical science's view that the world can be deconstructed and understood have produced a perception of organizational life and leadership that colors "every aspect of the way that we think about life," says Danah Zohar, management consultant, physicist, and philosopher.[11]

Scientific discoveries do not remain within the scientific community. They set in motion a chain of intellectual actions that soon escape into the world at large. As new insights from science propagate and reverberate across society, they become a part of our conscious and unconscious being, shaping our perceptions, intuition, and imagination. Early students of organization such as Frederick Taylor, founder of scientific management, found a special kinship with the deterministic and reductionistic nature of classical physics. They imagined organizations that worked like smoothly functioning machines and sought to design them. More recently quantum theory and chaos theory have captured the imagination of people in the fields of leadership and organizational development who had recognized the fallacy of viewing organizations as controllable machines and people as replaceable parts. People like Margaret Wheatley who are advocates for a more organic view of organization life pick up these insights and carry them into their writings and seminars, poets make intuitive connections between science and the soul, and theologians and philosophers use the revelations of science to revisit their thoughts about the nature God and humanity.

I am not a scientist. Like most of you reading this book, I depend on the work of others to learn about science. Margaret Wheatley's book was my first invitation to relook at nature through new eyes and to consider what wisdom it might offer as a guide to reimagining leadership and governance. A host of corporate leadership consultants, authors, and educators were early mentors, each pressing me in a different way to reimagine leadership and participation in governing boards. But I wanted more perspectives. The writings of Ian Barbour, Arthur Peacocke, and John Polkinghorne, each winners of the annual Templeton Prize for Progress in Religion for their pioneering work in advancing the study of science and religion, helped fill that need. Well-credentialed scientists deeply grounded in Christianity, they helped me more fully understand what Wheatley and others were talking about. Conversations on television and radio about science and religion, such as those hosted by Bill Moyers and Krista Tippett and conversations on science hosted by Ira Flatow,[12] have also been important guides through the maze of thoughts and perspectives that saturate our world. Together these people and the scientists whose work they discuss create a collage of insights that describe a natural world that is whole, relational, often paradoxical, saturated with information, self-organizing, open, and continuing to unfold. Karen Marie Yust, associate professor at Union Presbyterian Seminary, writes that the role of governing boards is to host the continuing conversation between the richness of their tradition and what it means to a witness to the creative, redemptive, and sustaining work of God in an increasingly complex world.[13] This is the same conversation Jim Collins and Jerry Porras, authors of *Built to Last: Successful Habits of Visionary Companies*, showed is critical to long-term success in the corporate world.

People live their daily lives in a world of identifiable objects, where distances are measured in metrics they can easily relate to, such as centimeters and kilometers, inches and miles, and with a single reckoning of linear time. We take this concreteness for granted; it is our context for perceiving and thinking about the world. For Christians, it affects how we encounter the biblical text and practice church governance. Over the past century, however, science has revealed a creation that includes an estimated 125 billion galaxies like our own,[14] spread over a universe conservatively estimated to be more than 20 billion light-years[15] in diameter, and where the smallest theoretical entity in the sea of subatomic stuff that makes up *everything* is estimated to be 10^{-33} centimeters in length.[16] Science also has revealed evidence of a rich history of creation measured in billions of years through the recession of galaxies in an expanding cosmos and abundant fossil records here on earth. Time also is not the absolute standard we experience but is, as Einstein's theory of special relativity demonstrates, inversely related to the motion and speed of the observer.[17] When I add to these revelations the counterintuitive nature and behavior of matter and energy revealed in the subatomic world by quantum physics and my personal rediscovery of the complexity of life in the natural world I knew as a youth, I can only respond in awe.

Awe is a word often lost in the business of governance. Science describes a world that lets us know in no uncertain terms that the control for which organizations strive is illusory at best. In his book, *Theory U: Leading from the Future as It Emerges*, C. Otto Scharmer says that the first step in effectively responding to change is to suspend our preconceptions about the nature of reality so that we can see what is really happening around and within us.[18] According to theoretical physicist Freeman Dyson, in later life Einstein said explicitly that anybody who did not approach science with a religious awe was not a true scientist.[19] As I seek to grasp the enormity and complexity of creation, I am certainly humbled, as I imagine Job must have been humbled when he was confronted by God's booming challenge (Job 38–39). Creation is so much more than our everyday life in the world of organizations, including the church, prepares us for.

Wholeness

Arthur Peacocke, one of the most influential scientists and theologians of the twentieth century, believed that the foundational observation from the Book of Nature is that we human beings are an integral part of a creation that is an unbroken whole. In his book

Theology for a Scientific Age, he observes, "Human bodies like that of all other living organisms, are constituted of the same atoms as the rest of the inorganic world and that to varying extents, these atoms also exist throughout the universe."[20] We are made up of the same *stuff* as the rest of creation. Atoms and the fundamental particles and interactions inside them are the stuff we share. The atoms that are a part of me as I write have not always been a part of my body nor will they remain a part of me. Peacocke continues, "The very iron atoms that enable the hemoglobin in our blood to carry oxygen to activate our brains . . . came into existence long before the Earth was formed and biological evolution began, and so before humanity appeared. Such is our affinity with the actual fabric of the universe."[21] Each of us is connected to everything else in the universe by virtue of the fact that all atoms are continually on the move from one entity to another.

But an even more profound level of wholeness is present in creation. Quantum physics tells us that electron pairs, which are a part of every atom, when they are separated remain connected regardless of the spatial or temporal distance between them. For years quantum physicists had theorized that such relationships existed. Albert Einstein, whose theories pointed to the likelihood of this phenomenon known as "nonlocality," had challenged the idea because he did not believe it was possible. But, in a 1982 experiment, French physicist Alain Aspect confirmed that elementary particles are indeed linked by unseen connections that operate simultaneously across time and space.[22]

My comments thus far about wholeness have focused on the atomic and subatomic level, but the same kind of wholeness is evident throughout creation. Peacocke sums up science's revelation well when he writes, "So during the twentieth century we have been witnessing a process in which the previously absolute and distinct concepts of space, time, matter, and energy have come to be seen as closely and mutually interlocked with each other," so much so that our ways of thinking about them have "to be superseded by more inclusive concepts of fields and other notions no longer picturable and expressible only mathematically." Peacocke continues, "Fortunately at the low energies, low velocities and small time and space scales ('low' relative to those needed to penetrate the subatomic world and 'small' relative to the velocities of light and the scale of the cosmos), the classical concepts continue to be adequate" for the majority of our daily lives.[23]

We do not need physics, however, to show us the wholeness of creation; evidence abounds in our everyday lives. All we need to do is pay attention to ourselves and to the world around us. Every two weeks during the summer months I witness firsthand how the countless "ownership" decisions about lawn fertilization practices, land use, and road construction in our county and neighboring jurisdictions determine whether life can exist in the streams of the watershed my wife and I monitor in southern Maryland. The myriad pharmaceuticals people and animals consume show up regularly in the groundwater monitoring program we help United States Geological Survey (USGS) teams conduct. Our interconnectedness extends beyond the boundaries of our county and state. Pollutants from the power plants along the Ohio River near my boyhood home in Indiana show up in our creeks and rivers in Maryland. Globally, what China does to curb the emissions of coal-fired power plants affects the environment in the United States. In the United States, the types of food people eat and government subsidies to farmers affect whether people in other parts of the world even have food to eat. The Internet, originally developed so that scientists working on important defense projects (like a number of projects I worked on) could share scientific data, now provides virtually anybody anywhere with the opportunity to instantaneously share virtually anything with the world. Cell phones and personal data devices give us the capacity to continually transmit imagery, voice, and data over the globe. Everywhere we look we see how interconnected we are. We are a relational and interdependent world.

Unique Identity

While we humans are an integral part of a whole creation in ways we are only beginning to see, we are also unique entities with distinct identities and characteristics. We have the capacity for memory, self-reflection, and reproduction. We have names, families, histories, personalities, and talents. There is abundant evidence that these same qualities exist to various degrees in all other living systems. This capacity of a living system to self-identify, adapt, and regenerate in a way that remains consistent with its established identity and its environment over time is a common theme in nature. It is often referred to as *self-referencing behavior*. Self-referencing systems adapt and regenerate by continually referring to themselves and their environment; hence, whatever forms these systems may take as they adapt will always be consistent with both their history and their current identity. Our DNA (deoxyribonucleic acid) guides the atoms that continually move through our bodies into the unique patterns that comprise both individuals and species. We are, it appears, both an integral part of the whole of creation and a unique entity within it. While such an arrangement may appear paradoxical, we continually must resolve the paradox in our consciousness. Danah Zohar argues in her book *The Quantum Self: Human Nature and Consciousness Defined by the New Physics* that the human capacity to continually self-reference, expressed in our consciousness, allows us to understand the experience of being both an individual and fully integrated into creation.[24]

Self-Organization

The Book of Nature reveals a highly ordered world with an astonishing capacity to continually organize itself, but the order revealed in the Book of Nature is not the type of order most of us who serve in organizations are prepared to see. The order in nature seems to be a fascinating, almost paradoxical mix of what might be viewed as order and disorder, with one continually giving way to the other to maintain identity and wholeness. Order at the subatomic level appears chaotic as particles appear and disappear into the sea of energy and information that constitutes space; the behavior of these particles is unpredictable and their identities are continually changing. This apparent randomness and uncertainty at the subatomic level evens out over countless events in such a way that, at the level of our everyday experience, objects hold their identity and behave in predictable ways.

The capacity within nature to continually self-organize is probably best illustrated in large-scale computer simulations of complex phenomena such as weather. These simulations allow us to witness the sensitivity of enormous complex systems to the slightest variation in their environment and the astonishing propensity those same systems display for sustaining a deep underlying order in the face of continuing change. Physical chemist and Nobel Laureate Ilya Prigogine's work with systems that classic thermodynamics would say will eventually exhaust their capacity to do work has shown that those systems can regenerate to even higher levels of self-organization in response to environmental demands.[25] We do not live in a world that is slowly running down, as the machine model of classical physics maintained; we live, instead in a world that appears to be continually unfolding in a manner consistent with its past and continually open to new futures.

How might one describe such a world? British medical scientist and environmentalist James Lovelock believes that the earth functions as a sort of supercomplex organism. His beliefs have come to be known as the Gaia hypothesis.[26] John Polkinghorne has likened the world described in the Book of Nature to "some self-regulating entity lying in between [something like the super complex organism imagined by Lovelock and the highly ordered elegant machine classical physicists imagined the world to be] for which we have no appropriate name to offer."[27] In our rush to divide and reshape creation into something we can use for our own interests, however, we have generally chosen to ignore the natural wholeness science is now witnessing in favor of a world that can be divided up and separately managed and administered for the benefit of the "owner." We develop and administer organizations to focus human activities to accomplish specific tasks more efficiently and effectively, whereas nature is ordered to promote the health and growth of the whole.

Information

To work as a whole, to preserve identity, and to continually evolve, the universe of energy and matter we live in requires the unrestricted flow of immense amounts of information about the identity and movement of everything present. Everywhere throughout our universe, tiny units of matter and energy are carrying and generating information as they interact and change from matter to energy and back. Organizations don't seem to work that way, however. Historically, we have treated information within organizations as a commodity to be carefully managed. Information is power. The more concerned we are with controlling specific outcomes, the more we seek to control the generation and sharing of information. But the type of information that lies at the heart of nature is not a thing that can be controlled; it is more like the blood that the ancients viewed as the source of life. This information guides the formation and movement of matter and energy throughout the universe; it gives order, prompts growth, ensures the continuation of species, and defines what is alive. Throughout creation information and matter are continually interacting. Because of the importance of information, Polkinghorne believes that information will take its place beside energy and matter as one of the primary components of creation.[28]

Theoretical biologist Stuart Kauffman demonstrated the importance of information to the capacity of complex systems to self-organize. Kauffman's investigations into the behavior of Boolean nets of connectivity, common to most digital electronics, showed how sharing only small bits of information can quickly enable a large system to more efficiently organize.[29] To visualize Kauffman's experiment, picture an array of ten thousand individual lights. Such an array would then have 10^{3000} possible on-off combinations of the lights. Kauffman set up his experiment so that every light knew whether two other lights in the array were on or off. As the experiment began, the lights blinked at random, but as the array continued blinking a pattern emerged that eventually settled down to cycling through approximately two hundred combinations.[30] Humans are infinitely more complex in their motivations and behavior than the binary lights in Kauffman's experiment. But the work management consultants such as Peter Block, Harrison Owen, and Juanita Brown have done with large groups demonstrates that people can also rapidly create order in the absence of structure through the simple process of talking to one another and continually sharing what was being talked about with whole group. Such processes, generally known as large group methodologies, are typically used to enlist people in developing new visions and pathways for organizations. But their potential is much greater if those who govern can get beyond the need to control and instead trust that people have the desire and capacity to discover the work that needs to be done and to do it.

Openness

The apparent openness and uncertainty evidenced in the behavior of matter at the subatomic level may be more challenging to many of us than any of the other themes discussed thus far in this chapter. We live in a world that appears to be so clear and reliable, filled with definable objects and incredible technologies that allow us to explore our solar system and peek into the universe beyond. Many of us believe that God is personally controlling the processes of our world along a predetermined path. How is it then that the behavior of particles inside each of the atoms that are the basic building blocks of creation is so "cloudy and fitful"?[31] Classical physics described the world as a great and wonderful machine slowly winding down as its finite capacity to do work dissipated. Quantum physics has added a "yes, but" to that view.

Quantum physics emerged from arguments about the nature of light. Scottish physicist James Clerk Maxwell appeared to resolve the question when he showed that light was a wave of electromagnetic energy. Later work by Albert Einstein and Max Planck, however, suggested that light could also be particle- or bullet-like. We now know, thanks to the work of English physicist Paul Dirac, that light can appear to be either wave or particle depending on how we choose to observe it. If we look for particles, we see particles; if we look for waves, we see waves. These early discoveries about the characteristics of light helped open the world inside the atom to our observation. Science soon recognized that the subatomic world was a great deal different from our reliable everyday world.

Before proceeding, I need offer a few comments on space. Contemporary science tells us that only about 5 percent of the vast expanse we see when we look toward the heavens is composed of objects such as planets and stars. The remaining 95 percent is thought to be composed of matter and energy that we cannot see, typically called dark matter (25 percent) and dark energy (70 percent).[32] Similar estimates tell us that approximately 99 percent of the space inside each one of the atoms that make up everything within the universe is empty space.[33] Assuming these calculations are credible, then everything we see and touch, including our bodies, is mostly space. Space to the classical scientist was a still, cold, empty, and silent void through which energy and objects traveled. Quantum theory tells us, however, that space is not empty; it is instead a virtually dimensionless sea of energy and information out of which particles are continually being born, existing for the briefest of time, then dissolving again into other particles and returning to the background sea of energy. Their masses, charges, and spins are conserved, but the number and types of particles are not constant. There is no familiar succession of events within the disturbed atom; no one thing causes another. Reality at the subatomic level is essentially a place where continuous potential is the norm.

The great metaphysical question posed by quantum theory is, what does the level of indeterminacy present in the subatomic world mean for our day-to-day lives? Two schools of thought have emerged within the scientific community. David Bohm, a theoretical physicist who also has made major contributions in the fields of philosophy and neuropsychology, has championed the view that beneath the apparent indeterminacy of the quantum world lies a deep, purposeful reality that is being incrementally revealed. Danish physicist Niels Bohr, who won the Nobel Prize for his contribution to the development of quantum mechanics, believed that quantum indeterminacy reflects a true openness to the future or in the nature of the world. The vast majority of scientists side with Bohr.[34] Does this mean that there is no objective reality, no predictable causal relationships, or chain of events leading to the end times? Is the world primarily a matter of perception, existing only in the minds of observers? These questions exceed the capacity of science to resolve. The wholeness of creation, the integrity of individuals, the continuation of self-referencing behavior, the capacity to self-organize, and the continual free exchange of information suggest that quantum indeterminacy is not simply some continuing lottery. The Book of Nature describes a rather finely tuned universe governed by physical laws that are neither too rigid nor too loose and a long and complex history that evidences a highly coherent yet imperfectly understood path.[35] John Polkinghorne urges that we remain respectful of the "veiling" present in the quantum world and not insist on the clarity we can often attain in the world of everyday phenomena.[36] He believes the observed openness at the subatomic level signals a fundamental openness in creation; it allows for much to occur through the workings of the Holy Spirit without violating the laws of nature.[37]

Locality

The themes I have been exploring emerge from the research of physicists and span the universe and time. Few of us can relate to the curved space-time described by the theory of general relativity or the fitful indeterminate world inside the atom. We are born, discover ourselves, make choices, hold conversations, feel love, form perceptions, develop relationships, and die in the world of the everyday. For us life is local, time is absolute, and size is measured in meters (or yards) rather than light-years or some virtually unimaginable numbers like the 10^{-33} used to describe the tiniest of hypothetical particles. While our lives are each localized within a specific setting in the everyday world, that localization does not insure that we know or understand a great deal about the natural world where we live. Eighty percent of the people in the United States now live in urban areas away from rural life and rarely experience it. A century ago, approximately 40 percent of people living in the world were urbanites.[38] In the massive rural-to-urban migration, we have lost both the intimacy with nature that most of our ancestors had and the ability to draw wisdom from it.

The science discussed above has also given us knowledge and tools to dismantle nature, disrupt its natural rhythms, and limit its openness. Our fascination with economic markets and big business, the artificial environments in which we live, our commitment to technology, our saturation in edited video imagery, and our preference for rapid means of travel further blind us to much the Book of Nature has to say about life.

Contemporary American poet and agrarian Wendell Berry
mourns our society's loss of intimacy with and responsibility for
nature. Berry writes about what we are doing to our world because
we continue to pay homage to classical science's view that our world
is a place that can be harnessed to produce wealth without regard to
the cost. Berry believes we cannot correct our excesses and abuse of
nature by technology administered through government and large
corporations.[39] I believe with Berry that we cannot continue to take
from the world or continue to rely on work practices that diminish
the human spirit, such as those that treat people as replaceable parts
in a machine without concern for the consequences. Historically,
business and government have relied on the promise of technology
to fix problems that very reliance has helped create. Experience
shows that technology cannot fix all problems. We must change the
way we live. The damages to the little watershed I help care for can
be repaired only by local action one field, one tributary, one stand
of trees at a time. Government regulation and funding help, and
technology is a valuable resource, but ultimately change must come
from people simply choosing to see the world as an interdependent
whole and living in harmony with it. Berry stresses the importance
of localness when he writes that the most "insistent and individual
concern of agriculture . . . is the distinct individuality of every farm,
every field on every farm, every farm family, and every creature on
every farm."[40] Seeing and valuing individuality requires us to live
locally in the present and to look around with loving awareness at
the impact our choices have on others and on the world on which
we depend.

Contemporary Science and Church Governance

It is ironic that the science of physics, which John Polkinghorne says is
by nature "methodologically reductionist,"[41] has helped us recognize
the highly relational and holistic nature of our created world. This
discovery has been the source of inspiration for a whole generation
of consultants, educators, business leaders, philosophers, church
professionals, and spiritual leaders who are calling us to reimagine

how we might better organize, lead, and govern ourselves in ways that build on these discoveries.

Too often we Christians miss the enormous contribution science makes in our lives by getting caught up in misleadingly simplistic and overly emotional debates surrounding evolution, climate change, and stem cell research, which continue to plague the church and polarize our society. The larger lessons from the Book of Nature get lost in the business of our lives and our convictions on the rightness of our perceptions and understandings. To many of us, nature is relegated to a well-landscaped church campus, attractive communities with parks and athletic fields, places to camp and boat, and vistas to be observed from well-maintained highways. Even those of us who deeply value the natural world sometimes lose sight of its wisdom and applicability to how we conduct the affairs of our church bodies and to the lessons in leadership nature offers. I am continually amazed at how many people I talk with cling to the classical science understanding of the world. The ideas emerging from contemporary science that I have outlined above are threatening to many. They often fear getting caught in the web of some New Age mysticism or the tentacles of Eastern religion if they take seriously revelations that the world is whole, relational, often paradoxical, saturated with information, self-organizing, open, and continuing to unfold.

Implications for Governing Boards

In her book *Finding Our Way: Leadership for an Uncertain Time*, Margaret Wheatley writes that our contemporary life in organizations is shaped by two stories.[42] The first story emphasizes structure, hierarchy, control, and predictability. This story uses the language of kingdoms and bureaucracies. Its proponents believe people need to be motivated and directed by authorities and that organizations need to be tightly managed to regulate behavior and ensure desired outcomes. This story found strong support in the reading of the Book of Nature that classical physics offered, and it closely approximates the *royal imagination* Walter Brueggemann described in his book *The Prophetic Imagination*, which I referenced in the introduction. The second story emphasizes the themes of relationships, wholeness, openness, meaning, and self-organization. Wheatley characterizes this story as a "tale of life" where "creative self-expression and embracing systems of relationships are the organizing energies, where there is no such thing as an independent individual, and no need for a leader to take on as much responsibility for us as we've demanded in the past."[43]

A number of years ago I became aware of these two stories' importance in how people frame organizational life. I love to take pictures. Each picture I take is *framed* in a way that includes and focuses on some things and excludes or blurs others. How we frame is the personal way in which each of us sees the world. The way we construct our frames filters out some things and allows other things to pass through. Frames help us order and evaluate our experiences and decide how we will respond; they also create blind spots and limit our imaginations. The ability to recognize how we frame things and to reframe or reimagine is critical to successfully responding to the challenges we face in life and those we face as governing boards responsible for the church's ministry. The vast majority of church leaders who participated in my dissertation research believed that most church governing boards operate out of the first story's frame. They believe governing boards whose members see leadership and organization life through the first story's frame are limited in their ability to discern God's invitation, to creatively respond to the needs of the ministries they are responsible for, and to model the type of communal relationships inherent in Paul's metaphor of the church as the body of Christ. I agree.

The Book of Nature is not prescriptive. It does not specify leadership styles or organization forms. It simply tells us how creation works and that we are an integral part of that process. If creation works the way contemporary science describes, then it would seem prudent that governing boards consider reframing their view of board life. This new frame would recognize the following:

- People (and their organizations) are an integral part of creation.
- All of creation is interconnected in profound ways.

- Creation is made up of countless unique entities that grow and continually change in ways that maintain their unique identity.
- Creation can appear to be paradoxical.
- Creation is self-organizing.
- Creation is dependent upon the continued free flow of information.
- Creation exhibits a powerful potential and openness to change.
- Ultimately, all life is lived locally.

Concluding Thoughts

Diogenes Allen, professor of philosophy at Princeton Theological Seminary, points out that in the early church God's rule was referred to as *oikonomia*, or "economy," the term used for the management or stewardship of the household.[44] *Household* referred to more than people who were related in a particular way or the way in which household affairs were administered; it included all of life in the place where the household was situated. When the ancient church thought about God's household—the universe—it included the natural world in which it lived. Creation was understood as God's great gift, a revelation of the invisible God that helped reveal God's power, wisdom, goodness, and creative and providential activity. I believe church governing boards should adopt a corresponding perspective. If we are to live out our mandate of stewardship, then we must understand what the Book of Nature has to tell us. But doing so requires that we intentionally set aside time in our governing boards to listen together to what the Book of Nature and the Book of Scripture have to say.

Science is seductive; its rational approach to recognizing and solving problems has proven to be a powerful force in our world. Still, while science offers many valuable insights, it is far from the complete or authoritative understanding of our world some would have us believe. Thus, while I believe people concerned with church governance must understand what science is revealing about the Book of Nature, we must also resist the tendency to rely too heavily on the rational thought processes of science and technology to interpret or respond to the deep political, spiritual, religious, environmental, sociological, and economic issues we face. I believe with John Polkinghorne that the more deeply science probes nature, the more it will discover realities that transcend science's abilities to understand.[45] I am drawn to theologian and biochemist Arthur Peacocke's belief that what unites creation is not something that can be rationally described using a formulation such as string theory. Rather, it is something more akin to the mystery of the relationship among the persons of the Trinity, and, at its core, creation is more sacramental than scientific.[46] Molecular biologist and Nobel Prize winner James Watson, who describes himself as "not religious," offers a similar conclusion after a lifetime of studying genetics. He concludes his book *DNA: The Secret of Life* with the observation that love is so fundamental to the essence of humanity that it must be inscribed in our DNA.[47]

J. B. Phillips, Bible translator and Anglican clergyman, wrote a book a number of years ago entitled *Your God Is Too Small*. In it Phillips argues that most people make God too small because we limit God to what we can conceive at that moment in time. In our zeal to be faithful and rational, we make God the product of our own limited awareness, processes of thinking, and imagination. The Book of Nature as physics and the natural world in which I live are revealing it, and they continually challenge me to look beyond my imagination in order to see what purposeful human activity centered in organizations, especially church governing boards, can be. My hope is that each of you would focus your attention on understanding the insights emerging from nature, especially physics, about how the world works and seek to discover together how those insights might inform the way you approach church governance.

4

Listening
to God

EFFECTIVE CHURCH GOVERNANCE REQUIRES MORE THAN knowing what the New Testament says about early church organization or what creation has to say about our relationships, and certainly much more than knowing *Robert's Rules of Order*, church tradition and polity, and how to manage organizations. To govern effectively within the church, leaders must first be able to listen *individually* and *together* to God. The primary task of governance is to *listen*. Dallas Willard, a prominent voice in contemporary Christian spiritual formation, emphasizes the primacy of listening to God in his book *Hearing God: Developing a Conversational Relationship with God*. Willard believes that although the Scriptures are God's written word, they are by no means God's only words.[1] We do not learn everything about God's desires for us from the Scriptures; rather, they are, in Willard's view, the foundation for an ongoing conversation. We must be able to listen to God in the warp and weft of everyday life to discern what God is doing and how we are invited to participate.

We do not hear God's desires for a variety of reasons. Perhaps the two biggest are that we in the church often fail to recognize God's real and continuing presence within and among us when we gather to carry out our governing roles, and we typically do not prepare ourselves to listen together. Instead, we seem more inclined to behave as though we are a collection of representatives assembled in our boards to hammer out some best course of action based upon our individual assessments of what is needed and the political, financial, and ecclesiastical pressures we feel. We apparently believe that opening and closing meetings with prayers, including devotions, when we meet; engaging in personal Bible study; professing the right beliefs; worshiping regularly; following parliamentary procedure; and using the best business practices to manage the institutional church's interests ensure that we are following God's call. We may even have full worship services featuring the best musical talent available, prominent speakers, and massive numbers of people participating—as denominations and judicatories so often do before, during, and after their regular meetings to set direction. But does that enable us to truly hear God? I wonder. Perhaps it helps, but increasingly I believe that the church, like all organizations, is limited in its ability to hear God's voice simply because we allow ourselves to be lulled into a pattern of business as usual. We assume we are following God's desires just because we are doing church work. To the extent that our capacity to consistently listen together to God is not developed, the church is unable to hear the fullness of God's invitation and robbed of its potential to be an agent for change in our world. Intentional listening helps us hear God's often subtle invitation to come and follow. If we truly believe that the Spirit is present and active throughout creation, seeking to draw each of us into a deeper relationship with God and to restore relationships with oneself, one another, and our world, then we must consciously try to *listen* with every fiber of our being for God's yearnings.

Listening, as I use the term here, is much more than recognizing some audible voice. Listening is directing every bit of one's mental, emotional, and physical attention toward something one wants to know. Lon Fendall, Jan Wood, and Bruce Bishop are Quakers who have served in a variety of leadership and consulting roles within the academic and business communities. They write in their book, *Practicing Discernment Together: Finding God's Way Forward in Decision Making*, "God communicates with us without words that we hear with our physical ears. The infinite God has an unlimited number of ways to communicate with us. We need to expand the language of 'speaking' and 'hearing' to include the wide diversity of God's many means of communication."[2] It took me a long time to fully accept that God was indeed continually present in my life and communicating in ways that transcended the more formulaic patterns of prayer and Bible study I had been taught were necessary to hear God. I wanted to be both reverent and businesslike in governance meetings, so I followed the formula I inherited, even though my personal prayer life was far more conversational and ongoing. Governing boards are usually skeptical of the benefit when I suggest that they regularly devote time to listening to God, because most people, including clergy, are simply unprepared relationally, procedurally, spiritually, and theologically to listen together to God.

The Books of Scripture and Nature tell us that creation is an incredibly complex and interrelated whole. Our world is designed to work together relationally to the heartbeat of a God of love. In Ephesians 4:15–16, Paul uses the metaphor of the body to describe how the whole church is connected, with Christ as the head, and grows in love as each part does the work it has been prepared for (Eph. 2:10). Sin fractured the unity of the world's design and continues to drive wedges among people as we pursue policies and practices of intolerance and exclusion that inhibit listening to one another. Our world is soiled because we have too often pursued our own interests and goals, however noble and right, without first listening to God. God is at work to redeem and restore creation. We have each been prepared for roles in that work, and it is our task to discern and live out that calling in ways that are often well beyond what our day-to-day life experiences prepare us for.

People everywhere are recognizing the importance of listening in depth to one another (and to ourselves) as the most effective means humanity has of finding new solutions to the countless problems our world faces. We often use different words to emphasize the importance of listening, especially if listening to *God* is important, but all are saying we must learn to listen in greater depth to one another and our world if we are to better address the continuing environmental, social, political, economic, and religious challenges we face. Listening is more than a skill for meeting social challenges, however. It is also a gift of great value that individuals give to one another. Douglas

Steere, Quaker scholar and leader in a wide variety of twentieth-century peace and humanitarian efforts around the world, captures the nature of this gift: "To 'listen' another's soul into a condition of disclosure and discovery may be almost the greatest service that any human being ever performs for another."[3] My wife and I occasionally have people into our home for several days of what we call *life planning*. Our guests' motives vary. Some are corporate executives with career questions. Some are seeking clarity around what they perceive as a call into a ministry. Some are weary church professionals asking, what's next? We are able to offer some wisdom that helps them make important choices, but mostly we offer them the simple gift of listening and reflecting on what we hear, and it is the gift of that listening that invariably opens their minds and hearts in astonishing ways.

How might you and I begin to listen together to one another and to God in our governing contexts? A friend frequently reminds me that Kurt Lewin, often considered the father of modern social psychology, said, "There is nothing so practical as a good theory."[4] I believe C. Otto Scharmer's *Theory U: Leading from the Future As It Emerges* is a good theory with enormous practical implications. Scharmer, who serves as a senior lecturer at the Massachusetts Institute of Technology, is a social reformer who focuses on helping business and nonprofit leaders develop more socially and environmentally responsible ways of organizing and carrying out their work. He believes people have the capacity to better address the ills of society and the world if we will simply listen together to the wisdom we have within and among us, and then work as efficiently as possible to convert that wisdom into action. His model—listening, determining a course of action, and then carrying it out—offers an important conceptual framework for those of us faced with the practical challenges of governing within contemporary North American church organizations.

The vast majority of the experiences people serving on church governing boards have involves what Ron Heifetz calls technical work. Technical work is work most people understand; we simply need to devote the resources and expertise. Church work is technical work. Church leaders and members know how to conduct worship services, offer Bible studies, set up food pantries, host small groups, run committees, manage church finances, and maintain facilities.

Even prayer, in its more formulaic forms, is technical work. People used to doing these more technical tasks often find adaptive work— in which the problem is unclear, the solution unknown, and the responsibility undefined—difficult to undertake because they lack the prerequisite listening skills. As a result, the need for adaptive work often goes unrecognized and the work remains undone until a personal, environmental, political, relational, or organizational crisis erupts. The crisis is then typically dealt with as technical work, and the cycle repeats itself. I suspect that many of the challenges the institutional church faces today are actually adaptive work that we cannot effectively deal with because of our limited capacity to listen *together*.

The left side of the U in Scharmer's model represents people's efforts to free themselves of the personal perceptions, attachments, and motivations that limit their capacity to truly listen to one another. This letting go or suspending is central to Eastern, Christian, and Native American spiritual traditions. It is usually described as an internal or downward movement and is necessary in order to create the opportunity for something new and different to emerge. The bowl at the bottom of the U is the open container in which in-depth listening occurs and new awareness and insight are nurtured. The key to the emergence of something new is a willingness to suspend judgment and engage in communal dialogue about what the participants in the process are hearing. Once a clear path begins to emerge, the emphasis shifts to the right side of the U, where formulating and enacting an effective and timely response is depicted as an upward movement.

Levels of Listening

Scharmer's typology describes four levels listening.[5] He begins with what he calls *downloading*. The vast majority of listening done in organizations is downloading; church governing boards are no exception. Downloading is the exchange of information about the day-to-day happenings in our lives. We are downloading when we give information about finances, buildings, attendance, and the miscellany of administrative and personnel activity. Downloading does not mean that weighty issues are not discussed; they are, but those weighty issues are typically framed in a way that the conversations remain focused on existing data about objects and processes. We are also downloading when we listen primarily for information confirming what we already believe. A good example is people in a politically polarized environment who choose not to listen to any information other than what supports their current point of view.

The second level of listening focuses on *gathering new information about objects or processes*. People listening at this level are open and often eager to adopt new ways of understanding, but the new ways invariably emphasize ideas and things. Most of my formal education, leadership training, and the Bible studies I have been a part of emphasized this type of listening. The third level of listening is empathetic listening. Scharmer calls it *listening from the heart*. The first two levels of listening are concerned with objective information about how things work and the way things appear to be. When people listen from the heart, they move from facts and figures about some concept, process, or object to another person's story and how he or she feels. People who listen from the heart are able to set aside their own agendas and listen to how someone else actually experiences the world. This type of listening embraces an intuitive sensing of people's feelings that often cannot be described, only felt. When we listen from the heart we can begin to sense the pain, anxiety, hopelessness, anticipation, and hope present in our world.

Scharmer's fourth and final level of listening occurs in the bowl at the bottom of the U. Scharmer calls it *generative listening*. Generative listening is a listening of the will. He uses the term *will* because he believes people must *intentionally* seek to let go of the perceptions and attachments that inevitably form when listening at the three preceding levels, because they limit the way people tune in to the world. Generative listening requires that we suspend our judgment about how things are or ought to be so that we can be more open to the potential that surrounds and fills us. In addition to suspending judgment, we must be fully present and engaged in the process and willing to be as open and authentic as possible. Generative listening is essential to addressing the challenges of adaptive work.

Generative listening is like the emptying of self and openness to God's leading that Christians have historically sought in their efforts to remove obstacles to hearing and responding fully to God. Christians often use the Greek word *kenosis* to refer to this process. Philippians 2:7 describes the emptying that Jesus underwent in becoming human: "[Christ Jesus] emptied himself, taking the form of a slave, being born in human likeness." Could that be our model? Such emptying is difficult because it means we must be willing to let go of everything that gives us identity, security, and credibility, but it is necessary if we are to truly hear. Early Christians were seeking the capacity to listen in this way when they moved from the urban environments of the ancient world to the deserts of the Sinai and from the courts and farms of medieval Europe to its monasteries and hermitages. But this level of listening is not the exclusive domain of the Christian monk or mystic; it is the level we all must seek if we desire to ground church governance in God.

Listening as Doing

There is yet more to listening, however. Listening also includes forming judgments, acting on those judgments, observing the results, gathering information on what happened when we acted, reflecting on the meaning of that information, and adjusting our behaviors accordingly. Acting on what we hear is an essential part of listening. Acting enables us to discover tangible and workable expressions of what we are hearing and to seek further clarity if what we believe we are hearing does not seem to be working or communicable to others. Scharmer identifies three levels of acting. They are, from the bottom of the U upward: crystallizing, prototyping, and performing.[6] *Crystallizing* is a birthing event that occurs when people begin to give form to what has been happening in their hearts and minds as they have listened together to their collective wisdom and call. Crystallizing is the "aha" moment when new windows of insight open and new paths appear. For Christians, crystallizing is the moment the desires of God's heart begin to emerge in some tangible form within us; it is analogous to the first step in the dialogue with God in *lectio divina*, when we offer our first understandings of what we believe we have heard back to God.

Once a path has become clear, a prototype must be developed to see if what listeners believe they heard actually works. *Prototyping* may involve a specific product, a process, or an organization. Prototyping becomes a way to continue to test what we believe we heard with real people in the real world. We prototype when we make models, draw pictures, try to write out what we are hearing, listen to what we say when we try tell others what we are hearing, and observe others' response to our words and actions. Often we go through multiple cycles of fabricating a prototype, modifying the prototype and trying again. The final level, *performing*, is actually offering a product or service to an entire organization or social group at a sustainable level and assessing how it works. If performing is a change in personal behaviors, then people embody it.

The sequence of actions from crystallizing to performing in Scharmer's model is not unique. What sets these actions apart from other descriptions of taking a new idea from concept to full implementation or production is how the actions are rooted. In Scharmer's scheme the actions emanate from a deep personal and collective listening by people who know who they are and have sought to fully embrace the potential they embody. Contrast this to actions in contemporary organizations that are simply the unchallenged continuation of past practices, the result of intellectual exercises, responses to social and political pressures, or driven by the pragmatics of economics. Even empathetic responses to the most pressing human needs can inhibit people from hearing God's voice, then addressing root causes and developing more lasting responses.

Some argue that such deep and collective listening is not practical or even necessary for most church organizations to succeed. Many congregations carry out high quality worship, fellowship, evangelism, stewardship, discipleship, and service that have a clear impact on people and the world without devoting any real time to truly generative listening. Many denominations continue to serve their constituents, train professional workers, and provide leadership for developing new ministries around the world. But might there be more? What might the church hear if we consistently sought to set aside our vested interests, cherished organizations, and specific roles and listened with open minds, hearts, and wills to God's yearnings for us today? Dallas Willard emphasizes that we need to listen more deeply to discover what is ours specifically to do here and now. If we don't continually direct our attention toward God and listen, how will we ever know?[7]

Richard N. Bolles, former Episcopal clergyman and author of the perennial best selling job-hunting book *What Color Is Your Parachute?*, frames our listening challenge well in another book, *How to Find Your Mission in Life*. He believes that all people have a mission, and each person's mission has three parts. Everyone shares the first two. They are "to seek to stand hour by hour in the conscious presence of God, the One from whom your Mission is derived," and "to do what you can, moment by moment, day by day, step by step, to make this world a better place, following the leading and guidance of God's Spirit within you and around you." The third is unique to each person: "to exercise that talent which you particularly came to Earth to use—your greatest gift, which you most delight to use, in the place(s) or settings(s) which God has caused to appeal to you most, and for the purposes which God most needs to have done in the world."[8] Because we each have a unique and personal gift and a mission, it is imperative that we continually listen to discern God's unfolding invitation to discover and use it.

But are we capable of hearing and understanding God's voice alone? We are social beings; we live in community. We need the continuing perspective of others, the Scriptures, and, yes, even the voice of the natural world in which we live to fully grasp our calling. Our individual listening is always imperfect and incomplete, but by continually seeking to do what we are hearing, and by observing what we are doing and how others are understanding and responding to it, we gain increased clarity and confidence that what we are pursuing is indeed God's call, or perhaps that what we are doing is *not* God's call. Bolles is writing primarily to individuals engaged in selecting a career; he implores them to look beyond a job to what God has equipped them for, but his thoughts and observations apply equally to groups of all types in settings of all types.

How Is God Present?

Models such as Scharmer's Theory U offer a way to envision and talk about complex subjects such as listening. They can be, as Lewin believed, especially helpful to people like me who have spent much of their lives in the corporate culture of America. But one's ability to hear God is also shaped by the image of God one holds. My former colleagues at Worshipful-Work, Val Isenhower and Judith Todd, cofounders of Water in the Desert Ministries in Albuquerque, New Mexico, highlight in their book *Living into the Answers: A Workbook for Personal Spiritual Discernment* the importance of the God images people hold.[9] Dallas Willard believes that more is involved than our image of God. He writes, "The idea of hearing from God is finally determined by who God is, what kind of beings we are and what a personal relationship between ourselves and God should be like."[10]

People's views of God, of what kind of beings we are, and of the nature of our relationship with God vary widely. The classical scientists I talked about in the preceding chapter tended to reflect the deistic view of God as the master clock-maker who set creation in motion and then stepped back. People who hold such a view today probably neither assign a great deal of value to listening nor worry too much about their relationship with such a deity, because their god is not actively involved in creation. People who believe God is a manipulator who controls our every move or a clairvoyant who knows the outcome of our every future choice and all its ramifications listen from another vantage. Envisioning the world through the lens of quantum physics suggests a more complex imagery. Is God a behind-the-scenes director who guides the great current in creation but not the details, a view quantum physicist David Bohm might support? Or is God a cocreator with humanity of a truly undetermined future, as the Copenhagen school of quantum physics, represented by Niels Bohr, might be interpreted to imply?

Most people I meet in church governance settings hold images that anthropomorphize God as a man, a powerful ruler, a benevolent sovereign, a shepherd, a parent, a judge, or a friend—sometimes bits of each. They typically see themselves the as subjects of a king, hapless sheep, little children, friends, actors, or citizens. In his book, *God and the World in the Old Testament: A Relational Theology of Creation*, Terence Fretheim, professor of Old Testament at Luther Seminary, makes the case for a relational God who has put us in a relational world where each of us has an important role that we alone can play.

Fretheim uses the Old Testament narrative to show that God endows humans with the Creator's image and places them in a unique role in relation to the rest of creation, one in which they share responsibility for the future of creation with God. True to character, God allows humanity the freedom and opportunity to become who they were formed to be and to experience the consequences of their choices. This commitment to share power and responsibility means that God then works through our choices. History is filled with the often tragic results of this freedom as humanity has pursued self-serving goals, but God has continued to allow us to choose freely. Fretheim goes on to say God's sovereignty should not be understood as divine control but as a sovereignty that gives to the created the capacity to influence creation. If God is indeed relational, then God is intimately interested in all facets of life, and God's caring permeates the entirety of creation, as Jeremiah 23:24 suggests, "'Do not I fill heaven and earth?' declares the LORD."

I find Fretheim's work informative. If we live in a relational world and God is a relational god, as I believe to be the case, then perhaps we Christians need to carefully assess how we think about conversing with God. Are our personal conversations with God open enough that we can hear what is important to God? When we gather as a governing board, do our conversations among ourselves and with God include our concerns? I suspect they do not. Willard suggests that we cannot hear God because of the way we view our conversations. He writes, "Our failure to hear God has its deepest roots in a failure to understand, accept and grow into a *conversational relationship* with God, the sort of relationship suited to friends who are mature personalities in a shared enterprise, no matter how different they may be in other respects" (italics added).[11]

As I am writing this, I am very aware of how my image of God as relational, my sense of identity in a highly interrelated world, and the personal relationship I have with God shape my listening. My family lived in a rural area in Southeastern Indiana when I was boy. Every year my parents put in a large garden filled with all sorts of vegetables that would hopefully feed the three of us for the year. Everyone I knew did the same thing. I am told that I was "working" in our garden from the time I could walk. I followed my parents, doing what they did. As I grew, I learned how to prepare the soil, plant, water, cultivate, take care of pests, harvest the various crops, and improve the quality of the soil we depended on for the following year. Together we cared for our garden and the trees around our home that offered pears, peaches, cherries, and apples; they provided much of the food we ate. The work was hard, especially the long hours of backbreaking weeding and picking beans in the summer heat. But it's not the hard work I remember most; it is being with my mom and dad doing something meaningful. I still have the sprinkling can I used to lug water from our cistern to water new plants and, on occasion, to alleviate the effects of long dry spells. I also have the little blue and white enameled bucket that I carried when I climbed our cherry trees to pick their fruit.

I did not come to understand my parents' wishes overnight. I learned by imitation and repetition. As we worked together, I listened for specific instructions on how to carry out the various tasks involved, but I was also hearing who they were as people, what brought them joy, what they were anxious or concerned about, and what was expected of me as a member of that family. When we were working together in the garden, we talked about all kinds of things. Conversation helped break the monotony and take our minds off our tiredness, flies, and the heat. In the beginning I was always there with Mom and Dad; as I grew older I often worked alone. While I was physically alone, however, I felt their presence reminding me to "do it right."

Along the way I became aware of another presence—God's. God was there with me in the hot sun between the rows of lima beans and corn. This wasn't just the God I learned about in Sunday school and vacation Bible school or heard preached from the pulpit each Sunday; this was God. God was not there alongside me, as one of my parents might have been. God was around and in me. We talked about many things, often about my fears for my mother's health during several illnesses. The God I came to know there in the garden on the east side of our old house on a hilltop over looking the Ohio River was neither a god who told me how to live nor a god to whom I continually went for guidance or for healing. We were simply there together; sometimes we "talked," sometimes we didn't. As I grew older, that God remained fully present. But as my life filled with the demands of family, career, and church, I too often invited God to take a seat in the back row while I attended to the sea of other faces surrounding me whose demands for my time always seemed more important.

Almost six decades have passed since the first garden conversation with God. I am keenly aware of how those encounters have shaped my listening and have guided my life. In those early years I followed my parents to learn how to participate in our family's life. At some point I began to seek to follow God to participate more fully in "the divine life." Elizabeth Liebert, dean of San Francisco Theological Seminary, says, "Participating in the divine life means doing what the divine life does, and that is creating. . . . If the goal of our life is union with God . . . then when we are united with God, we find our fulfillment by participating in this creative activity."[12] Our garden provided food each year until my parents' careers and my activities in high school no longer allowed time to garden, but the experiences there with my parents have continued to feed me, and the conversational relationship with God that began in the stillness of those rows of plants has become the center of my life.

For people who serve on governing boards to participate in the creative activity of the divine life, they must learn to listen and act at all the levels Scharmer outlined. This means that they must be able to listen for both the day-to-day stuff necessary to run an efficient organization and the heartbeat of God amidst a world of opportunity and deep pain. In his book *A Testament of Devotion*, Quaker scholar and spiritual guide Thomas Kelly talks about this challenge. He says, "There is a way of ordering our mental life on more than one level at once. . . . On one level we may be thinking, discussing, seeing, calculating, meeting all the demands of external affairs. But deep within, behind the scenes, at a profounder level, we may also be in prayer and adoration, song and worship, and a gentle receptiveness to divine breathings."[13] If we are to truly participate in the divine life, then we must be able to order our lives as Kelly suggests and be prepared to listen together, free of our preconceptions and attachments. The way Christians have historically sought to do that has been through the practice of spiritual disciplines.

Spiritual Disciplines

Over the centuries, people who have hungered for a more intimate conversational relationship with God have evolved a set of practices to help them better recognize the presence and voice of God and to understand what God was saying. These practices, or spiritual disciplines, help us listen for God amid the voices of our everyday world that clamor for our attention, action, and resources. Spiritual disciplines when practiced within church governance help church leaders move away from our fixation with the business of the church, our fascination with facts and objects, and our dependence on the work of the mind. They help us better listen to our own lives, the lives of others, and the world in which we live and offer ways in which we can align our lives more closely with the heart of God. By themselves, spiritual disciplines cannot change people, nor should they be viewed as ends to be sought. They are simply a trusted way for people to more fully listen to and share in the grace of God. Richard Foster, theologian and founder of Renovare, lists twelve spiritual disciplines in his book *Celebration of Discipline: The Path to Spiritual Growth*: meditation, prayer, fasting, spiritual reading, social mercy, solitude, simplicity, submission, worship, confession, spiritual guidance, and celebration. These disciplines offer a way for us to move beyond the materialism, fear, and self-focus that permeates our culture toward being more Christlike. The disciplines are gifts, but to grow through them, we must practice them in our personal and group life. As we do, they will help us turn toward the energy and rhythms of God— God's timing, God's vision, and God's call.

Some contemporary Christians look back toward the first-century church through idyllic eyes and see a people much more attuned to spiritual disciplines than we are in the church today. I can't adjudicate the truthfulness of such a claim, but I can certainly understand how the pressures of contemporary life diminish their acceptance in our world. Foster acknowledges this challenge when he offers the opinion, "It is hard to overstate how saturated we are with the mentality of popular science."[14] While writing this chapter, a clergy friend and faithful practitioner of the traditional Christian spiritual disciplines Foster identifies has been vilified by a small group of people in his denomination who believe that prayer must conform to certain preordained verbal models clearly rooted in the approved doctrines of their faith tradition. His church body, like others, harbors well-organized and highly vocal groups of people who fear anything they cannot define and control, and the prospect of individuals living in a conversational relationship with the Creator outside the controlled environment of the institution's polity and established doctrines and practices frightens them. Their fears are justified. Robert Wuthnow, professor of sociology and director of the Princeton University Center for the Study of Religion, writes in his book *After Heaven: Spirituality in America Since the 1950s*, "The point of spiritual discipline is not to encase the soul in rigid rules *but to give it room to maneuver and to grow*. When it is rightly understood, the sacred is always too powerful to be tamed by simple formulas and techniques. But spirituality also requires practice, a serious engagement with the sacred that moves one beyond the realities of everyday life" (italics added).[15]

As I followed my parents around our garden doing what they did day after day, year after year, I did not become bound in a burdensome routine. Quite the contrary; I found the freedom and encouragement to grow in the discipline I learned from them. Sure, the work was hard, and many days I would have rather been almost anywhere else, but the discipline I developed there in that Indiana soil has informed my life, and I return to those images and experiences regularly with the eagerness of a person longing for a good conversation with a dear friend.

Spiritual Discernment

As we listen to God, we often find ourselves faced with the prospect of choosing from among many what-appear-to-be-good alternatives. How should we proceed? Which alternative would God most desire us to choose if we are to truly be a part of the divine life? *Spiritual discernment* is the term Christians have traditionally given to this task. Many people talk about God's will in connection with discernment. I prefer the word *call*, however, because it seems to better capture what Elizabeth Liebert terms "the open, relational, and non-predetermined nature of God's relationship with us."[16] *Discernment* comes from the Latin verb *discerno*, which means "to separate, to distinguish, to determine, or to sort out." Historically, Christians have used the term *discernment* to describe the process of identifying the Spirit at work in one's life and what that Spirit is leading them toward. Liebert says, "Discernment, then, is the process of intentionally becoming more aware of how God is present, active, and calling us as individuals and communities so that they can respond with increasingly greater faithfulness."[17] Clearly, some people are especially gifted in discernment. They are people of wisdom who seem to have a special ability to hear God's voice amid the other voices clamoring for our attention. Thomas Kelly refers to these especially gifted people within the Society of Friends as "weighty friends."[18] But discernment is much more than a gift some people have received; it is an art and a skill that all of us, individually and together, must learn if we are to understand and follow God's call.

As I have sought to discern God's desires for my life, I have experienced God to be an ever present inviter and a relentless pursuer in the placid places and the turbulent currents of my being. In response, I have felt both the need to yield and an invitation to continually exercise a greater level of personal initiative. The psalmist's words "You hem me in behind and before, and you lay your hand upon me" (Ps. 139:5) express what I feel: I am both trapped and free. Looking at my life, I notice many times when God has simply said, "You choose," and walked with me while I agonized over the choice. In contrast, at least three times I have experienced something I usually describe as being thrown from my horse on the road to Damascus, recalling Paul's dramatic, life-changing encounter with God on the road to that ancient city. Other times God has used what some people refer to as a "third thing" to open me to a path I could not have otherwise seen. A third thing is an object, event, or another person whose presence draws attention in such a way that a new insight emerges, one that could not have been gained directly. There have also been times when I have simply felt the need to back off from a course I was pursuing. Such times have typically been accompanied by a concurrent invitation to remain still or to move toward something else.

I am in the midst of yet another time of turning now. As I write these pages, I sense that God is inviting me toward something that I cannot yet identify. Indeed, most of my spiritual journey has been spent moving toward something obscure yet somehow compelling. In the past when I have not understood, I have sought to simply say yes and to press on until a door closes or a stronger invitation appears. Quakers refer to this following a path that unfolds as "way open." Looking back over my life, I can see a number of career paths that have opened that I have sought to follow. It took awhile for me to recognize that my career was not my life. God had something in mind for me apart from a traditional job or profession. I was being called in a way I had no words to describe or models to observe. When I have been invited to remain still and wait, I have been blessed with peace and anticipation as well as questions and doubt. At times, the invitation to be still has come with the need to prepare. Such times of stillness and waiting have involved living fully in the present but without a vision of what the future may be. During those times I have occasionally been haunted by visions of what might have been. Where might I be if I had stayed in the defense industry, the environmental sector, or as a church administrator? But God has always provided, so each day I simply try to say yes. Can we be sure we understand God's beckoning? My rational mind continually questions my listening; my heart sometimes joins it. Looking back I realize that most of time, had I been permitted to "know," I would not have understood or perhaps even said no. Maybe the best we can do is to try to continually listen with our entire mind, heart, and will. Somehow, I believe that is all God wants.

Corporate Spiritual Discernment

The church's rich tradition in spiritual discernment is primarily focused on our personal search for God's call. I cannot remember encountering the term *corporate spiritual discernment* in the context of church governance until my future mentor and friend, Chuck Olsen, introduced me to it in the mid-1990s. By then Chuck had coined the term *discernmentarian* as an alternative to the more familiar role of parliamentarian. He was offering a four-day program at Worshipful-

Work's facilities in Kansas City, Missouri, that was designed to help people in church governance listen to God together by integrating the practices of worship, biblical and theological reflection, storytelling, visioning, and spiritual discernment into their meetings. The Quakers and various religious communities such as the Benedictines (especially Benedictine women), Franciscans, Marianists, and Xaverian Brothers have histories of corporate spiritual discernment. Not so with the rest of the church, which has generally pursued a more hierarchical and bureaucratic process for evaluating courses of action and relied on parliamentary procedure to conduct its meetings.

While corporate spiritual discernment languished within the church at large, "vision" became highly prized. Our fascination with vision parallels the importance assigned to it by people studying leadership in the business community. Generally speaking, students of leadership tell us, successful leaders are people who have a clear, compelling, and well-crafted vision for a preferred future that others can easily relate to. When I first became involved in developing leadership within the denomination I belong to, we sought to equip clergy and lay leaders with the *vision*, skills, insights, and technologies that those who studied contemporary business and church organizations told us were necessary for success. The courses we offered were much like those offered in the business leadership programs I participated in, except they were, in the words of a friend, "baptized." *Baptized* generally meant recognized church leaders presented the material, began the presentations with prayer, offered occasional devotions, used religious language, and on occasion sang hymns or religious songs. Some participants in our programs did develop a compelling vision that captured their people's imagination, and their congregations showed improvements in measurable ways. Those leaders and their congregations became the stars. Many, however, could not put together a compelling vision or "sell" it to their congregation, and they often saw themselves as lesser leaders by comparison.

Vision is important; it enables people and organizations to focus their energy and resources. Proverbs 29:18 reminds all, "Where there is no vision, the people perish" (KJV). But my concern is, what lies behind the vision? Is it the people's vision or God's? Many visions of church organizations are solid biblical visions; they embody the best of our church heritage and meet the needs of our neighbors and our world. But are they rooted in God's calling to us now, and how would we know unless we continually practice listening to God together? Virtually every board I have been associated with in any way has assumed that God's call to them was essentially a continuation of what they had always done: preach, teach, administer the sacraments, care for the sick and dying, offer opportunities for fellowship, and with varying degrees of intensity spread the good news to the unchurched and care for the poor. Is that it, or might there be more? Some people rationalize away their responsibility to listen to God by assigning that function to clergy or the church hierarchy. But does God only speak to clergy and those higher up in the church "chain of command"? Does God also speak to people who serve on governing boards? If God speaks to people who serve on governing boards, does that conversation occur before meetings so that they can then take that word they received to the governing board meeting? Or, does God speak to the assembled group in a way that transcends God's communication with individuals? Does God simply say yes or no to specific questions, such as whether to proceed with a building program or close down a ministry or accept or decline a call? Is there more involved? There is no one answer to these questions, and that is the point. God is not limited by organizational boundaries or defined roles. God speaks to each of us and is an eager participant in any gathering if we will simply listen.

I need to understand and live out my call. My congregation needs to understand and live out its call. Both require discernment. My personal discernment requires all my attention. Memory, intuition, relationships, prayer habits, the Bible, my religious beliefs, awareness of my body, my reason, and the natural world in which I live all have a role in my discerning God's call. Groups seeking to discern their call must also be open to such a diverse means of listening and discerning. Because of the importance of following God's call, the primary goal of every governing board of any church organization must be to discern and live out its call and to encourage, equip, and enable the people it serves to do the same. We are simply to be open to God in the fullest possible way and then to obey.

Many people understand the importance of discernment, but evidence suggests that most congregations do not practice or encourage it. Presbyterian pastor and author Graham Standish believes that church leaders must make discernment the cornerstone of their personal lives and seek to influence the community they serve to do the same. I agree. Ephesians 2:10 NIV says, "For we are God's handiwork, created in Christ Jesus to do good works, which God prepared in advance for us to do." The first priority of any group within the church ought to be to focus all of its personal and corporate attention on learning what good works God has prepared for them, and then doing them. I believe that anything congregations do that is not in accord with God's leading is potentially wasteful, and whatever we undertake that is in accord will likely succeed, regardless of how difficult or improbable it appears to begin with. I am not saying that God cannot work in all things or that our best efforts to live out God's call are not thwarted by the evil that is loose in the world. I am saying that we waste a lot of people's precious time and resources in our churches going through the motions of ministry because we have always done it this way or that.

If church governing boards do choose to focus on discernment of God's leading, then they must be open to the possibility—I would argue, probability—that God will lead them and the church organizations they serve to face a host of issues that are wider, deeper, and longer in view than they have previously faced. As such, we who serve in governing roles within the church must continually seek to listen more intently to the world we are so interconnected with. To better understand the desires of God, governing board agendas must be built around prayer *together*, biblical and theological reflection *together*, listening to the voices from our world *together*, and discernment of God's desires *together*. Doing these things by ourselves is important, but when we pray, reflect, listen, and discern *together*, we open ourselves to levels of mutual understanding and shared insight that extend beyond what we can do individually.

I first recognized this a number of years ago when I was leading *Crossways*, a two-year intensive study of the Bible. As the class evolved, our conversations moved to how each lesson applied to our context as Lutherans in southern Maryland. We talked about the text, carefully listened to one another, prayed together, dreamed about new ministries, and asked a great many critical questions about who we were and what we were called to be. Within a couple of years, many of the people from our class had been elected to our congregational governing board. The prayer we practiced, the relationships we developed, and the in-depth biblical study and theological reflection we had shared helped us to work through some major issues that I don't believe we would otherwise have been able to recognize or act on as effectively as we did. Few boards have the opportunity that the *Crossways* class afforded, but a great deal more can be done to better prepare people to serve in governing roles than what most church organizations ever even appear to contemplate.

Introducing corporate spiritual discernment into an established culture, especially one as entrenched and as bureaucratic as the culture that ensnarls much of the contemporary North American church, can be a real challenge. Corporate discernment does not come easily. It is a foreign process to many people who have been thoroughly schooled throughout their life in the importance of getting things done, and it requires time. Discerning God's call together requires a level of listening many of us have never experienced. It requires a spirit of openness and willingness to try something new. *Strong leadership* is necessary if corporate discernment is to be a priority, *careful coaching* all along the way is required to do it well, and *continued encouragement* is essential to help people overcome the inertia present in each of us and the church system we are a part of. The pressures to abandon discernment and focus on the familiar and the day-to-day tasks of administering the church's business are strong, and, as the next chapter will discuss, even the best led and most carefully planned and supported efforts quickly fade as soon as any of these three elements is allowed to wither.

Incorporating spiritual discernment into church governance requires a type of leader different from those most of our church organizations have rewarded. When a group focuses on listening to God, leaders become less agenda setters and decision makers and more witnesses to and stewards of what God is revealing within the group. Karen Marie Yust, at Union Presbyterian Seminary, writes, "When church committees constitute themselves as bodies for discernment, God becomes an active participant in their decision making process. God is worshiped, engaged through prayer, and sought as a founding partner in the realizing of God's realm. God's presence on committees changes them from business groups concerned primarily with practicality, frugality and efficiency to spiritual discernment groups determined to be good stewards of all God's gifts within the congregation."[19]

As Yust suggests, successful leadership in a community intentionally seeking to discern God's desires looks a great deal different from the more business-oriented style of leadership that often flourishes in a typical twenty-first-century North American church bureaucracy. When I served in the highly action-oriented structures of the US Air Force and later as a senior executive in the business world, I was expected to make decisions, usually quickly and often in ambiguous situations, about the people, programs, facilities, and equipment I was responsible for. My professional life was geared to rapidly sizing up the situation and acting decisively. I carried those role expectations into a series of leadership positions within the church, where they were continually affirmed. I still live with the instinct to quickly size up situations and do what I believe needs to be done, especially when I know people look to me to point the way and when the organization seems to bog down if I don't. I suspect that there are many people like me who simply don't realize there is another way of working in organizations.

When church governing boards commit themselves to corporate spiritual discernment, however, they are saying they believe that over the long run, groups of people have a greater capacity than individuals, however gifted they may be, to listen to and discern God's desires, and that the experience of groups discerning together offers the best opportunity to develop the gifts of each member. We are each called to the simple vocation of listening and yielding to our Creator's desires in this highly interconnected and interdependent world. Yielding allows God to work through us, and as we yield, we create the opportunity for others to discover and develop their unique place. To the extent a church governing board is unable or unwilling to yield and it exerts its own desires, it skews the wonderful diversity of opportunities to serve in God's world. It values gifts and reward behaviors that address a relatively narrow band of needs, those primarily focused on the economic returns essential to sustaining an organization. As it does so, it marginalizes many gifts and eliminates opportunities for others to even be discovered. Most groups find that it takes more time to work through important issues when they focus their attention on discerning God's desires together, but as they commit that time something quite profound begins to happen. They find the time gives them new life; it increases the organization's capacity to listen more deeply and to respond more creatively and authentically to continually unfolding challenges and opportunities.

Discernment helps governing bodies focus on the right things. Too often governing boards spend their time together on tasks that are relatively unimportant yet generally measurable, while fostering a culture of discernment is relegated to the back burner. As a practical matter, nothing should be done in a meeting if it can be done elsewhere. Precious face-to-face time needs to be focused on building trust among board members; listening with their minds, hearts, and will; discerning God's call together; and drawing on the collective wisdom present to carry out the work they are called to do.

In her book *Coming to Consensus*, Jill Tabart, a medical doctor and architect of the Uniting Church in Australia's transition from a traditional bureaucracy to a church body focused on corporate discernment, talks about what the transition in her denomination required. The transformation began when the church body began to grapple with the question, "What sets the church apart as an organization from secular institutions in determining the outcome of deliberations?"[20] Tabart describes how her church body decided to pursue corporate spiritual discernment, the challenges they faced in doing so, and what they learned. She lists the lessons the denomination learned under four categories. Three of the four deal with the details of the chairperson's role and what she terms the functional and practical aspects of making sure everyone is included—designing agendas, selecting venues, and a host of other details necessary for everyone to fully participate. The fourth category is what Tabart calls the *theological basis*. She says:

- Corporate discernment is theological.
- God has a way forward for the church.
- Reliance on the guidance of the Holy Spirit is essential.

- All people are gifted and in need of each other to function.
- Each person's contribution deserves respect.
- The Spirit's voice speaks even through those with whom you disagree.
- You must be willing to risk and accept unexpected outcomes.[21]

The task of the Uniting Church in Australia's leaders was not easy. Tabart makes clear that implementing corporate discernment on a denominational scale requires prayer, biblical study, theological reflection, and a lot of difficult relational and planning work. Proponents of corporate spiritual discernment often neglect the critical planning and relational work Tabart says are so important. They seem to believe that discernment is God's preferred method of governance and people need to get in line. If implemented from that perspective, corporate spiritual discernment is reduced to the level of any other top-down change within a bureaucracy and robbed of much of the benefit it can offer the church. Integrating discernment into the governing structure of an existing institution filled with people who have thrived in that culture is a complex task. Failure to recognize that complexity will mean that efforts to introduce corporate spiritual discernment into the governing culture of a congregation or other church-related organization will likely fail.

Graham Standish, in his book *Humble Leadership*, identifies the qualities of the leader he believes are necessary for this work. They are humility, self-awareness, commitment to a life of prayer and seeking alignment with God, the capacity to see unity amid division, and the willingness to plan and work toward specifics while remaining open to God's possibilities. Standish concludes his book with some practical steps for people in leadership roles who seek to introduce corporate spiritual discernment:

- Surround yourself with good leaders and let them shine.
- Elicit ideas, seek God's guidance, and set direction.
- Give guidance and let go.
- Accept criticism, resist offense, and provide support.
- Become thankful.[22]

What Standish describes is not a linear process but a circular movement that continually evolves over time as people grow spiritually, the community changes, and new leadership emerges.

The most frequent fear I hear voiced by people in church governing roles is that integrating spiritual disciplines, especially corporate discernment, into the board's work will blunt the cutting edge of any agenda or push away decisions that need to be made. I understand that fear. Those of us who have spent our lives in organizations know the pressures to get things done. We are action-oriented people who intuitively grasp what needs to happen and do it. I have a friend with a long record of success in business who has served with distinction on countless church boards, but he absolutely refuses to participate in any board activities that are not focused on making decisions and implementing them. Church organizations welcome such people because they bring efficiencies that are often lacking. The vast majority of the things people do together within the church are things that need to be done, and we know how to do them. These are the tasks my friend excels in leading. He gets people involved and produces a quality product on schedule. If a church organization believes, however, that God desires for them to extend beyond what they are currently doing, perhaps in a whole new direction, then they need to listen together with mind, heart, and will to discern God's full invitation.

What assumptions have we in the church made about the capacity and motivation of people and the work to be done within the church if we fear discernment will blunt any agenda or postpone necessary decisions? Corporate spiritual discernment assumes people are motivated, are uniquely gifted by God, and, if given the opportunity and encouragement, have the capacity to work together toward something as meaningful as pursuing God's call together. If people believe they do not have the capacity or time to involve others in discernment or believe that the knowledge or moral position of one group is superior and needs to be imposed on the whole, then discernment, or any consensus-based process, will likely not work.

Relying on corporate discernment forces a congregation or other church body to confront still other assumptions they make about the value of people and what is important in the church's life. Corporate spiritual discernment looks forward from the present. Most corporate discernment models lead participants to a place where they must choose among alternative paths. By what standards might we judge the positive and negative aspects of a particular course of action, however? As I pointed out in chapter 1, organizations have a long history of assigning a higher value to things that can be quantified and measured in economic terms. Such measures usually offer insights into the continued economic viability of the organization. Organizational health is important, and every governing board must be concerned with it, but we need to be clear about how the organization's health relates to who we are as a congregation or a denomination and what we are called to be and to do. If we focus on organizational health measures, are we also prepared to see the value of the hundredth sheep or the sparrow that Jesus used to illustrate the scope of God's concern? Do we ask if we are growing in love for our neighbor and in kindness, generosity, gentleness, and self-control? Are our thoughts and actions drawn toward what is true, right, pure, lovely, admirable, excellent, and praiseworthy? Are joy and peace becoming more hallmarks of our days? Are we living in a manner consistent with our core identity? Do we feel alive in Christ? Are we nurturing our capacity to recognize, receive, and share God's gifts? How different these latter questions are from more economic measures of merit that proliferate in institutions. What resists quantification can only be gleaned through sharing our stories, and sharing our stories may require us to listen to each other in a way that evokes the disclosure and discovery Douglas Steere believed is so valuable.

Decision Making

Ultimately, all our listening and discernment within a congregation, denomination, or other church organization results in specific decisions. These decisions trigger the action steps on the right side of Scharmer's U. Some of our decisions signal major policy changes and have far-reaching effects. Others are simply small incremental movements along an established path. The choices we make, taken together, make a significant statement about who we are, who we perceive God to be, and the nature of our relationship with God. They are our theology in its most concrete form. Luke Timothy Johnson, Professor of New Testament and Christian Origins at the Candler School of Theology, talks about the importance of our choices and how we make them in *Scripture and Discernment: Decision Making in the Church*: "I think there ought to be a connection between what a group claims to be, and the way it does things. The church claims to be a community of faith; is there any connection between this claim and its actual communal life? This could be tested by looking at several places where churches express their life, but a particularly important and revealing place is the process of reaching a decision."[23]

The decisions made in church governing boards are about far more than simply doing the business of the organization. They are, as Johnson believes, a fundamental statement about the nature of God, the character of the church, and the faith we purport to hold. If, as the familiar expression goes, actions speak louder than words, then our decisions and the process we follow in reaching those decisions define us. Johnson asserts that the work God is doing and has done among people of faith is the most vivid picture of God we have. If God's work offers us the clearest understanding of God, then the church must continually seek to discern what God is doing and adapt its self-understanding accordingly. Johnson says,

> The key element in decision-making as a theological process—that is, an articulation of the church's faith in the Living God—is discernment. Discernment enables humans to perceive their characteristically ambiguous experience as revelatory and to articulate such experiences in a narrative of faith. Discernment enables others to hear such narratives as the articulation of faith and as having revelatory significance. Discernment enables communities to listen to such gathering narratives for the word of God that they might express. Discernment enables communities, finally, to decide for God.[24]

If we follow Johnson's line of reasoning, then the church can move forward with meaning only to the extent it shares its faith stories, because they speak to what God is doing in the community. Sadly, the story too many church organizations tell is what the clergy and different groups within the organization are doing for the organized church. What might the church look like if we were willing to set aside attachments to our collective bureaucracies and gather ourselves around what God is and has been doing among us in our daily lives? Do we have any idea what God is doing among us? What might we learn if we actually sought to listen to our individual and collective stories apart from organization filters we impose? Who would we talk to? Knowing the stories of the people within our organizations is often difficult in today's world, given the diversity and mobility of our society. Members do not share the years of interwoven lives that were so much a part of the family I grew up in and the first congregations I attended. Yet our collective stories are important. It is only through listening to God together and to one another's stories that we can begin to learn what God is doing among members of our community and often in us. Our stories, discernment, theology, and faith are intricately interwoven and all rooted in listening to God. If such listening is important, and I certainly believe it is, then we need to focus time, attention, and resources on it.

Concluding Thoughts

I can't begin to guess the number of times I have heard people I considered to be mature Christians who are serving on governing boards say that God answers our prayers with either yes, no, or not yet. And so they offer petitions hoping for a yes, preparing alternatives if they receive a no, and living in the midst of a host of not-yets. Is that all there is to listening to God? We ask, and God gives us thumbs-up or thumbs-down, or we act without God's input all? Do we think God might be interested in being invited to the table throughout our deliberations, not just to bless what we have already decided or are about to vote on? The God I know wants to be involved from the beginning in all aspects of our personal and corporate lives. Most of us understand the importance of communicating within our communities about more than the information and ideas necessary to sustain the basic processes of organizational life. If board life is to be more about the life and calling of the organization and the people it serves, then the board must also allow space for the new to appear. Many truths, insights, and discernments are not likely to emerge from groups gathered to receive information, share new ideas, or listen to one another's stories. Rather, they can only emerge from within a group gathered simply to listen, as Scharmer advocates, to whatever comes in their silence.

At a particularly critical point in the life of the Worshipful-Work governing board, one of our eight members who is a Quaker suggested that we simply sit together in silence for one hour. During that time, we were each asked to listen to the Spirit's leading within ourselves and to try to sense the Spirit's movement within the group. We had the opportunity to speak once if we chose. Some felt led to offer a brief thought; some did not. At the end of the allotted hour, we understood the course we were to take and all agreed. Imagine such a process with your church council, session, or board of directors at a particularly difficult time. It has taken me a long time to learn that being still together can be a way of hearing profound truths that often resist being verbalized. A simple plaque on the wall by my prayer chair bears the words from Psalm 46:10: "Be still, and know . . ." Wow! What a strange concept in our very verbal, 24/7, sound-bite society. Knowing can come through stillness. It can and does, if we will but listen and discern. Together, listening and discernment bring the blessing of awareness and the call to act.

For some, discernment is a definable task to engage in when the gravity and complexity of a situation transcend our ability to analyze events and determine a course of action. If this is your view of discernment, it's a start. We can certainly use various discernment processes to help us make specific choices. However, discernment is fundamentally a way of life, a decision to continually seek God's desires and to live them into being every moment of every day. As discernment becomes the focus of our individual and corporate lives, we are able to see God's presence in the basic fabric of the highly relational world in which we live. Our personal and corporate spiritual senses become more acute, and as they do, we will learn to see God's creative and redemptive presence in more areas of our own lives, in the lives of others, and in our world. We become more comfortable with stillness, and we listen not to acquire knowledge but to hear our God and the world we have been given to care for and develop. And we are able to act more clearly and decisively because we know who we are and what God has indeed called us to do.

The type of listening I am suggesting in this chapter is not new. Christians have sought and developed it over the millennia, especially in the more contemplative traditions; and contemporary academics and consultants working with business leaders have said it is necessary if corporations are to reach their potential. If in-depth listening is so important, why is it that members of church governing boards who are so often influenced by the corporate world appear so reluctant to listen to what leading thinkers in the corporate world are telling them about the importance of listening?[25] Why is it also that governing board members who profess such a deep desire to do God's will are resistant to dedicating time to listen together with open minds, hearts, and wills to the call of God? My experience suggests that it is because we find it easier to live at the top part of the U Scharmer defines—where we are free to go about business as usual without having to face questions from others about what we do and why we do it.

In a lecture entitled "Holy Obedience," Thomas Kelly writes that spiritual maturity brings simplicity rather than the further complexity and the busyness one might expect. This simplicity is implicit in Jesus's summary of the commandments, "'Love the Lord your God with all your heart and with all your soul and with all your mind.' ... And ... 'Love your neighbor as yourself'" (Matt. 22:37–39), and his continued admonition that we are to become like little children. Such simplicity emerges only when we center our lives on what is truly most important. Kelly explains, "The amazing simplification comes from when we 'center down,' when life is lived with singleness of eye, from a holy Center where the breath and stillness of eternity are heavy upon us and we are wholly yielded to Him."[26] It is this place of simplicity of purpose and clarity of call that governing boards must seek, and the only path to it is listening together and yielding to God's call.

5

Voices of
Experience

PEOPLE SEEKING TO HELP CHURCH-RELATED GOVERNING
boards become more intentional in listening to God together face
formidable challenges. Four major obstacles stand in the way of most
efforts. The first is the vocal and often assertive group of people who
value being right (whatever that means to them) and often appear to
have little interest in listening to the differing views of others. They
forcefully argue that they know God's will and are commissioned to
compel compliance and shun those with whom they disagree. The
people participating in the research that serves as the basis for this
book often refer to these folks as "fundamentalists," but they note
also that others on the liberal end of the spectrum can be just as
dogmatic about their values.

The second obstacle is the entrenched bureaucratic and
hierarchical structures within the church that resist change. Over the
years, people come to know how their particular organizations work
and how they can manipulate them to their advantage. They may
not like them, but they understand what goes on and why, and what
they can do about it. In addition, many church leaders have worked
hard to get where they are within "the system" and are reluctant to
risk losing what they believe they have earned and their power to
influence what the organization does.

The third obstacle is simply the culture of *Robert's Rules* that "fundamentalists," "liberals," and everyone in between relies on every day. We are accustomed to voting, to majority rule, and to winning and losing by a set rule first prepared by General Henry M. Robert in 1876.

The fourth obstacle is that clergy and laity alike are simply unprepared, either in their formal training or in life experiences, to do discernment together. We understand how to make decisions and to propagate them, and we understand majority rule, but we don't understand listening to God together.

Despite these formidable barriers, many people appear to be looking for an alternative to the ubiquitous bureaucratic and majority-rule governance models that dominate church life. The desire for something more spiritual than what we are accustomed to transcends denominational lines and faith traditions. This desire is what gave birth in the mid-1990s to Worshipful-Work, a nonprofit organization dedicated to integrating spirituality and administration in church governance. The founders of Worshipful-Work believed that the church had been given many gifts to enable it to better listen to and creatively respond to God's desires. From the time of its inception until it transferred the last of its assets to Water in the Desert Ministries in 2008,[1] Worshipful-Work offered a variety of forums at its home offices in Kansas City, Missouri, and in other venues around the United States and Canada for people to learn about corporate spiritual discernment, develop networks of like-minded men and women, and share their yearnings and experiences with one another. I was fortunate to serve as a member of Worshipful-Work's governing board for eight years.

In July 2006 Worshipful-Work hosted its final gathering at the Upper Room in Nashville. The gathering was entitled "Spiritual Discernment as Gracious Space: Sharing, Experiencing, and Exploring the Deep Joy of Communal Discernment." This invitation-only event brought together thirty-three church leaders from eleven Protestant denominations and the Roman Catholic tradition for four days to share their learnings and their dreams and to listen together for God's leading. The dialogue was exceedingly rich and informative. Fellow board member Steve Doughty—a retreat leader, author, and former regional denominational executive in the Presbyterian

Church (USA)—later wrote that the four days offered "one steady and connecting tone: joy."[2]

During the decade of its existence, Worshipful-Work touched the lives of thousands of people in congregations across the United States, Canada, and a number of other countries. The Nashville gathering provided a glimpse of Worshipful-Work's influence and the status of communal discernment in the contemporary North American church. In anticipation of its closing, I had asked my colleagues on the Worshipful-Work governing board to allow me to use the organization's database of people who had been involved in various training events. I wanted to study what those people had experienced when they tried to introduce spiritual practices, specifically corporate discernment, into church governance. After almost two decades of experience in leadership development in a variety of denominational and large independent church venues that drew heavily on learnings from business, I had come to feel something important was missing from the leadership programs typically offered. I knew others shared my perceptions, and I wanted to know what they had learned. To pursue my questions, I enrolled in a doctor of ministry program at United Theological Seminary, where I studied the connection between the contemplative traditions of Christianity and the attention to spirituality emerging in academia and the business world and explored how church governance might profit from a better understanding of what was occurring in both arenas.

The work began with a Quaker-type clearness committee made up of the other members of the Worshipful-Work governing board. Their role was to help me discern whether a study of experiences of people who had shown a commitment to communal discernment in church governance was, in the words of one our board, "mine to do." The idea behind the clearness committee is simple. Quakers believe that within every person is an inner light that the individual needs to be able to access for guidance. Perhaps the best way of accessing the wisdom of that inner light is through the questions of others whose goal is to draw forth this inner wisdom from the person engaged in discernment, rather than advising them. My committee's careful questioning allowed me to see that studying the learnings of people who had participated in Worshipful-Work events was indeed "mine to do." We agreed the then upcoming (July 2006) Worshipful-Work collegium would offer an excellent opportunity to refine the scope and direction of my DMin study. Along with Steve Doughty and another person from outside our group, I listened to participants throughout the four-day collegium and prepared a summary of what was heard. Following the collegium, the Worshipful-Work board helped me develop nine open-ended questions designed to draw out the learnings of people around the country who had demonstrated a commitment to introducing spiritual practices into the governing boards in their church organizations.[3] I sent the questions to 105 people, and 78 offered their written responses. Those responses and the "listenings" from the Nashville event are summarized in this chapter.

Altogether the experiences of 111 people contributed to this research. The participants were divided almost equally between men and women. While most were clergy or members of religious orders, a significant lay voice is also present. (Appendix A provides more detail on this distribution.) The participants served in thirty-one states and represented eighteen Protestant denominations, the Roman Catholic tradition, and Judaism. (Note: More detail on denominational affiliation and state of residence is included in appendixes B and C respectively.) Their stories are incredibly diverse, yet they are drawn together by the common longing to help the church be more intentional in listening to the desires of God's heart and less concerned with the business of being an institution. (Note: I have retained references to *the church* to simplify my reporting here even though two members of Jewish congregations contributed to my research.) Some people who contributed to this work had been actively seeking to reform church governance for many years; others had just begun. Some had succeeded; others had not. Some had served as bishops, denominational executives, social entrepreneurs, church consultants, authors of books and materials on church life, and senior pastors; the rest were active as lay leaders in denominational or congregational roles. All participants were "insiders" who have served the institutional church faithfully. Each had served a long time in the trenches of church governance. Together they offer a perspective that embraces life in mainline Protestant denominations, the Roman Catholic tradition, and Reform Judaism. They spoke in slightly different ways about the obstacles they faced in their various roles, the openness they encountered in different groups and settings, and what they learned from trying to encourage members of church governing boards to listen to God together. I hope I have been faithful in reporting their experiences and to the spirit in which they shared them.

Unique Qualities Present in Participants

As I listened to the people gathered at Nashville and read the responses to the nine questions I sent out, I recognized that there was something about these people that I had not often found in church governance. Steve Doughty used the word *joy* to describe the spirit of those gathered in Nashville. Joy is an excellent start, but also present were other qualities that I have struggled to succinctly define without unfairly generalizing or appearing critical of others who do not exhibit the same behaviors. Let me summarize what I felt after reading and rereading every response I received from my survey questions, listening to participants in Nashville, and rereading the summaries of the Nashville event.

Participants often contrasted themselves to "business types." They recognized the importance of those spiritualities rooted in logic, order, consistency, and decisiveness that business types often embody, but they stressed the importance of mystery, feeling, intuition, reflection, and discernment in understanding God's leadings. The people who offered their insights to this work also tended to see the goodness in people more than their faults. They emphasized faith over certainty, love over fear, potential over risk, and freedom over control. Where others saw scarcity, they saw abundance; where others sought data, they were drawn to story; and where others valued expertise, they valued self-directed learning. The people whose experiences are described here emphasized the need to be stewards of all of creation and exhibited openness to truths emerging from people different from themselves. Indeed, they expressed a special frustration with people with what they viewed as closed minds. Participants seemed to be able to lift themselves above the political, theological, and practical differences in church operations that divide the church to focus on drawing ever nearer to the heart of God. Finally, while they recognized the need for operating efficiencies within the institutional church, they were first and foremost committed to listening to God together.

Motivations for Seeking Change

Virtually every person whose views are incorporated in this book believes that the governance model so common throughout the church, which draws heavily on the experiences of North American business and the parliamentary process, is inadequate for the challenges church governance faces today. A few of the people surveyed accepted the existing model's shortcomings as the best we can do; the vast majority did not. Those in the former group work hard to help people make the best of the system they have. Those in the latter group have sought change, because they believe the models most church bodies rely on to govern themselves are not adequate for the difficult and potentially divisive issues confronting the church. For the most part, those who have sought to be a catalyst for change have been frustrated by their experiences; some have been emotionally and spiritually wounded. Discernable levels of bitterness and disillusionment were also present.

The participants critical of common church governance practices believed that governing boards are simply too secular, and they voiced their discomfort with being part of a church body that goes about its business with little or no apparent effort to learn first what God desires. They believed that the behavior of governing bodies within the church ought to reflect the basic teachings of their faith and that, in most cases, it does not; and they expressed a hunger for something more. They reason that governing bodies within the church ought to reflect the love and unity in Christ that the church preaches. However, many believe church governing bodies do not reflect that love and unity. They believe how we govern ourselves says more about who we are than what is preached from the pulpit. One participant described what is apparently a common experience, especially in congregational governing boards, and how he felt about it:

Once the opening prayer was ended, God was sort of excused from the meeting while we got down to business. God's presence during the meeting was pretty much ignored until we had taken care of "business." . . . If God's presence and blessing were going to be invoked at the beginning of the meeting, then that presence needed to be acknowledged and called upon during the meeting as well.[4]

Many participants believed the governing board experience could be a real opportunity for people to experience listening to God together and working more efficiently to follow God's invitations. As they voiced their beliefs about what governing boards might become, they did so with a passion for the spiritual growth of the people they served. They hoped that as the governing bodies in their congregations and other church organizations began to listen to God together, people could begin to see that walking with God in this complex and interrelated world involves far more than the immediate needs of the organization on which so many governing boards focus.

Personal Spiritual Practices

All of the people participating in this research believed strongly that their personal spiritual practices were at the root of their desire to incorporate spiritual practices in church governance, and that you cannot advocate what you do not know or practice yourself. The absence of personal experience was my problem when I first sought to introduce spiritual practices into my congregation or talk about them in my judicatory role. I had found something that felt extremely valuable, and I wanted to make it happen. The problem was that my spiritual practices did not include any time for discernment; I was a take-charge person still living in the awareness and imagination of the business culture that had dominated my professional and church life. I was not a credible advocate for the spiritual practices I sought to introduce. Regardless of how well crafted my words were, how reasoned my approach, or how skilled my presentation, I had not walked the walk.

The people participating in this study have practiced various spiritual disciplines and have sought to share their experiences with others. They have dared to introduce change within denominational, congregational, and professional power structures. Their comments are rich and clear: personal practices shape corporate practices! One participant explained, "My own spiritual practices played a huge role. . . . I had used individual discernment for years. It was what led me into ordained ministry. It informed all of my major decisions. Without that foundation, I don't think I could have ventured into corporate discernment with any level of comfort." Another observed, "Without a living [spiritual] practice personally and communally, there is no light to share." There are no short cuts. Without an authentic spiritual life rooted in the spiritual disciplines of prayer, solitude, discernment, reflective Scripture reading, and so forth, it is a waste of time to think about embarking on such practices within a church or any other organization. Likewise, once you begin to shape your life around these spiritual disciplines, it becomes increasingly difficult to participate in governance and administrative processes that ignore them. Once the participants in this study had tasted more, they were increasingly resistant to settling for less. They deeply believed that the pain experienced in their church bodies could be resolved if leaders simply made seeking God together their focus, rather than an occasional afterthought.

Introducing spiritual practices into church governance is not simply about introducing a new way of doing business; it's about wholeness—about living an undivided life. One of the participants argued that people of faith cannot live their private and corporate lives differently. "It's about living the undivided life, walking the walk, integrity of being and doing. . . . I truly believe that while human experience of God is personal, it can never be separated from the corporate/communal. . . . To me that implies that spiritual disciplines/ formation must be intentionally engaged corporately." It took me awhile to get the message that any change needed to begin with me; I needed to grow in ways I did not yet know existed. My church life had emphasized knowledge and efficiency; I sought to model them. At both the congregational and the judicatory levels, I had taught, presided, led worship, and achieved a level of proficiency in a host of other tasks that I thought were important; but introducing spiritual practices was something different, and I was not prepared for the task.

Tradition and Culture

The tradition and culture of congregations and denominations appear to be reliable indicators of a group's receptivity to incorporating traditional Christian spiritual practices, specifically communal discernment, into its governance and administration. Some participants in this study believed their denomination or congregation was unreceptive to the introduction of spiritual practices because the group's original spirituality had somehow been lost to the larger culture's business and parliamentary traditions. One participant's response captures the type of governing board tradition and culture that can blunt efforts within a congregation to listen and discern together:

> I was always frustrated that board meetings, Lutherans call them council meetings, were organized by secular and business standards, though they were supposed to be the body that directed the spiritual work of the church. It was a dichotomy that always bothered me, since we could discuss money and building problems but anything spiritual was left up to me, the pastor.

Participants believed that helping people connect with the founding spirituality of their denomination or congregation can be important to the group's ultimate receptivity. They opined that many people, especially in the Protestant traditions, simply do not understand terms like *spirituality* and *spiritual practices* in their contemporary church context. They simply do not have the history and language to naturally embrace traditional spiritual practices, especially in corporate settings. As a result, spiritual practices are often rejected out of hand as too Catholic, charismatic, mystical, or New Age. Participants also felt that congregations whose primary emphasis is on conversion are less likely to practice discernment, because those congregations tend to see less need for the practice. They believe that God's call is clear, and that churches need only to organize and get busy evangelizing. Since the business model has been developed to get things done as efficiently and economically as possible, it only makes sense to use it; hence the strong tie often evident between large congregations and business innovations.

Time Pressures

The people who shared their experiences and insights both at Nashville and in responses to my questionnaire believed that dividing life into dichotomies of sacred and secular, assuming that board service is restricted to managing or directing the business of the church, and especially placing increased demands on people's time create expectations that work against incorporating and sustaining spiritual practices in governing boards. They spoke with an implicit sadness about the potential for a richer, fuller life that is lost because of the way the church defines and lives out its corporate life. Frustration and deep disappointment were expressed by so many as they envisioned what might be if church governing boards could see themselves concerned with the work of the church and not simply with doing church work. One participant commented, "Folks worry about taking the time for spiritual practice. Some live compartmentalized lives—believing spiritual practice is for worship, while the session or council should be concerned with business." Another observed, "I think that the major resistance to incorporating spiritual practices is a concern to keep the meeting as short as possible, so that participants will be able to go home and spend time with their families."

The challenge of incorporating spiritual practices into church governance is not simply the culture of the church, however; it is also the time pressures of the larger culture in which we live. People who serve on governing boards and in administrative roles live busy lives often made even busier by the pressure to continually give more time to the institutional church. I used to cringe at a pastor I knew who lived by the maxim that if you wanted something done, you should ask a busy person to do it. Participants continually stressed the need to help people be better stewards of their time. Sabbath rest is a foundational element of the biblical narrative; the church needs to practice it in our organizations and help people make it a part of their lives. We get too caught up in doing good things and fail to devote time to understanding what God is inviting us to do.

C. Otto Scharmer emphasizes the importance of both stillness to listen and acting with speed and efficiency, but he also emphasizes that listening should precede action. Some people, especially people in business who have developed the capacity to see clearly and respond quickly, intuitively grasp what they believe needs to be done and see no need to spend further time thinking before acting. Others require time to understand a situation before they respond. The challenge to the first group is that the presenting issue may not be the real problem or a problem that ought to be quickly resolved. The challenge to the second is that some things may need to be done quickly and decisively for the good of the community. My heart saddens when I listen to stories of nominating committees who tell candidates that serving on a congregational governing board will require only a few hours of their time per month. Good governance is important and requires time to listen as well as the capacity to act. Participants repeatedly stressed that when we in the church minimize the importance of governance, we are cheapening a critical function and undermining our ability to be good stewards of gospel message and the gifts of the people who live the gospel into being in their day-to-day lives.

The Role of Leaders

Participants in this research were generally dissatisfied with what they perceive to be the clergy's and lay leaders' inability and unwillingness to take the lead in integrating spiritual practices into governance and administrative settings. Their observations about this reluctance and inability among clergy correlates with Urban Holmes's observation in *Spirituality for Ministry* that clergy may lack the spiritual focus and discipline necessary to provide effective leadership.[5] The participants in this study were generally pessimistic about clergy's desire to work with people in discernment and to risk their role as "expert" within the church structure. Observed one participant, "One very big factor boils down to the willingness/openness of clergy to this way of doing things. If they're not willing, it's pretty much a lost cause." Lay leaders were also viewed as generally unreceptive to introducing spiritual practices into church governance. Advocating such a change is often a tough position for a layperson to take. Participants believed lay leaders who are willing to take a stand and push back against other lay leaders who value "efficiency" over "spirit-based decision-making" are difficult to find. For spiritual practices to become part of the governing and administrative culture, skilled, consistent, persistent, and supportive leadership is essential. Without a sustained, well-focused approach involving both clergy and lay leaders, it simply won't happen. A survey respondent noted, "The number one foundational issue is the attitude of the spiritual leader. Of secondary importance, though not far from number one, is the competence of the leader in incorporating the practices within the organization. A highly qualified and positively motivated leader will overcome almost all other obstacles." Another participant in this study wrote,

> Integration of spiritual practices thrives when leaders step into their own leadership position of power and invite others to "come along" and see what good things await them from God. It is my experience that integration is modeled from the leader as being a part of his or her own life, not simply a task that is an agenda item. I, personally, have never experienced resistance to this notion.

If spiritual practices are successfully introduced, the next challenge is to develop a new generation of leaders who will embody, encourage, employ, and sustain them. Where participants in this study were able to institute spiritual practices, most appear to have been progressively abandoned once the person or persons who introduced them had left the scene. One participant observed that integrating spiritual practices into church governance "requires both clergy and lay leadership who have the vision for boards guided by spiritual principles, knowledge of ways this can be expressed, skill in utilizing these practices, and persistence to recommit to this way when things start drifting back toward traditional ways." Another commented,

> After my time as president, it didn't take long for them to disappear.... Clergy still supported them, but people who followed in key positions wouldn't buy into them . . . and there was a fairly rapid turnover of presidents . . . who didn't have the interest or willingness to continue on.

Developing and equipping the next generation must always be a concern. Again, this takes time and commitment and a more systematic program of leadership development than many church organizations have the interest in or capability to do.

Generally speaking, participants believed that the people within the church lacked the basic insights and the skills needed to participate in church governance where spiritual practices were important, neither were they equipped to practice them in their own spiritual lives. They believed people who served on governing boards need to be able to reflect more deeply on emerging issues in the world around them than they seemed able or willing to do. They believed governing boards and other church groups had a limited capacity to integrate spiritual practices into their work together because they lacked an intellectual understanding of basic theological concepts such as grace, baptism, and images of God and the ability to reflect theologically in corporate settings. Participants emphasized that people cannot embrace something they do not understand, especially if it appears to challenge their core beliefs on how organizations should work and what role laypeople should have within the institutional church.

Participants also believed that business and parliamentary models are so dominant in our society that they will continually reemerge unless they are consistently countered. These models are further reinforced by Bible stories repeated within church education programs and sermons that emphasize people in authority, hierarchies, conquests of territory, the construction of buildings, and the acquisition of territory and wealth. The result is that people see few if any organizational models where communal discernment is regularly practiced. To many respondents, this disparity in everyday use between the more familiar business and parliamentary models and an approach that emphasizes communal discernment is the major impediment to change. The people participating in this study used a variety of terms to attempt to describe this difference. Some respondents contrasted *business* and *spiritual*, others talked about ecclesiastical community deciding institutional issues and a covenant community seeking God's will about God's work. A few spoke in stronger language that included phrases such as "white male domination" in contrast to something often unnamed but implicitly more egalitarian. A number of people expressed the belief that people might better understand the contrasting approaches to governance if congregations relied more on a spiritual formation model versus Christian education. In their view, as one participant expressed it,

> We need to broaden what we have typically called Christian education over the years (too much emphasis on "information") and talk about what we are doing as Christian formation. Formation . . . provides for opportunities to learn about and engage in spiritual practices as well as to learn about the faith.

The idea of Christian *education*, however, is deeply engrained in the psyche of the church. We tend to be a rational people; we have, as I pointed out in chapter 1, a "head" type of spirituality. We typically describe our faith in terms of the beliefs we hold and differentiate ourselves from one another based on carefully crafted statements that generally minimize God's more mystical qualities in favor of those that can be well defined. Meanwhile the spiritual practices that embrace the unknowability of God and teach faith in a more experiential way are at best viewed as the result of our beliefs rather than an integral part of faith's formation.

Openness and Resistance

The roots of openness and resistance to incorporating spiritual practices into church governance extend beyond the culture and traditions of the congregation and denomination. Participants cited a number of different settings where they had experienced openness to the integration of spiritual practices. These included Sunday worship experiences, large and small groups in judicatory and congregation settings, judicatory staffs and task forces, congregational meetings, business meetings, visioning and planning groups, search processes, youth groups, congregation governing bodies, women's groups, women religious, and among seminary students. They also cited a number of settings where they had consistently experienced resistance. They were large groups, congregations, church councils, "every" governing body, judicatories, and seminary administrations. Participants clearly felt that while there may be some difference in openness or resistance in specific organizational settings, the real determinants lay in other variables. In general, the more emphasis on mission and spiritual formation present, the more likely spiritual practices will be accepted; the more a group is focused on managing finances, buildings, and programs or sustaining specific traditions, the more likely spiritual practices will be resisted.

Participants believed the following factors helped create openness to introducing spiritual practices both in congregations and in denominational settings.

- A capacity for trust and intimacy
- A spirit of hospitality
- An emphasis on visioning
- A concern for important life issues and healing
- A belief that the work was important to the mission of the church
- A recognition that what the group had been doing was not working and that options appeared to be limited
- A culture of learning
- A strong leadership core focused on spiritual formation

One participant observed, "There is openness at every level in every place if you give it time and work to develop the climate in advance. Developing a culture of learning is important." Another reported, "My experience has been that larger administrative gatherings are more likely to include spiritual practices than smaller ones. I think that part of this is that the larger meetings often involve more preplanning and may be better organized." Participants appear to agree that the more importance people in the church assign to governance and the more attention they pay to agendas and preparing board members for the issues the board needs to consider, the more likely spiritual practices will be positively received.

Participants cited the following as factors that increased the likelihood of resistance to the introduction of spiritual practices:

- The principal focus is on material and programmatic issues.
- There are personal agendas and close-mindedness to anything else.

- There are prescribed ways and traditions for how things are to be done.
- The view of ministry is relatively narrow or is focused on social activity.
- The people are cool toward one another and unsure about community.
- Spirituality is seen as a gimmick, a fad, or equated to the charismatic movement.
- The group is averse to risk or fearful of loss.

The following quotes are typical of the responses I received when I asked where people were most likely to resist the introduction of spiritual practices:

- "People who are in areas of leadership where their 'business' experience is used . . . (such as finance, trustee, council chair, etc.) resist it, because they feel inadequate to be able to lead in this area."
- "I find the most resistance in places where persons have become polarized and almost frozen in their positions on an issue, or are desirous for their own agenda/side to be victorious on a given issue."
- "Churches with the most resistance are those who confine talk of faith to worship and Sunday school, who have leaders who don't see themselves as spiritual leaders, who don't understand the importance of trust and who have not explored their images for God."

Participants also spoke of resistance from district superintendents, pastors of large congregations, and bishops who appear to be protecting the existing system.

By the time they arrive at these career levels they usually hold different values of leadership than are featured in prayerful discernment. They were not equipped by their seminary educations to function comfortably in prayerful discernment. They were taught that power in leadership comes by being in control—and "being in the Holy Spirit" means that another is in control. I have personally found a surprising level of confusion about what spirituality and spiritual practices are.

Congregational health is closely associated with openness to the spiritual practices discussed above. The capacity for trust, community, and patience; the willingness to listen deeply to one another; and the desire to know the heart of God were believed to be solid indicators of congregational health. One person said, "I believe the most foundational issue is relational trust. Unless you trust that the others involved in the process with you have your life and faith at heart, it is difficult to be vulnerable enough to engage in any significant spiritual practice." Another addressed the primacy of the health issue this way: "Healthy congregations will be more spiritually focused and foster more spiritual practices in the life of the congregation. Unhealthy congregations, congregations experiencing high levels of anxiety, are focused on reducing anxiety; so they are impatient and want quick fixes, which results in diminishing the importance of spiritual practices."

Anxiety is a powerful motivator, and the prospect of a quick fix is seductive to many board members as they seek to minimize the time required to carry out the board's responsibilities. Anxious people are impatient, and it is difficult to coax them into the slowing necessary to listen. They want resolution, they want it now, and they want it on their terms. Anxiety and the desire for a quick fix lure us away from the deep listening to one another and to God that is necessary for a healthy community.

Some years ago I was invited into a congregation near my home that was beginning to polarize along familiar biblical-interpretation fault lines. Many people recognized that the opposing positions, if pursued, would eventually divide the congregation, and they wanted to avoid a split. But the leaders on either side were resistant to listening to anyone who was not sympathetic to their increasingly rigid positions. I had just joined the Worshipful-Work board, and I believed that some of the practices I had learned there could help the congregation, because I knew people on both sides and recognized that they each wanted to be faithful to God's calling. I suggested introducing prayer, biblical and theological reflection, listening to one another's stories, and communal discernment into their uberbusiness and rigid parliamentary-style governing process. They received my suggestions politely and said no, preferring instead to continue to fight among themselves with the political tactics and rules they were familiar with in an attempt to win their point. The final split wounded many people. While I felt that I had failed them, the real lesson for me was recognizing just how difficult it can be even to talk about the idea of introducing spiritual practices into governing boards when the board or congregation is not healthy.

Planning and Evaluation

Participants emphasized that the people responsible for conducting the meetings and setting agendas must, before governing board meetings, better formulate issues and think them through more deeply as well as pray about them. The importance of careful preparation and evaluation at each step of the process was continually stressed. One person talked about what is required: "Constant prayer. I have found that developing agendas in a manner following the worship order and also to have theological rationale with items and asking others to develop theological rationale for their work has been helpful." Another stated,

> The pastor's own vision of Jesus as head of the church and the church board
> is essential. His perceived need to be "in control" of time and topic issues
> limits growth of this culture. His hard work to prepare the decision makers
> to understand all the issues prior to the meeting opens the way for adequate
> time for the informal interjection of prayers, hymns and stories.

In general, participants believe that more time needs to be spent in governing bodies on fewer more-important and foundational issues, and that identifying and properly preparing to address those issues takes time. Introducing spiritual practices is clearly a foundational issue. Participants continually stressed that unless people in positions of leadership were willing to help board members understand spiritual practices, specifically corporate discernment, why it is important, and how the change will affect them, spiritual practices will probably fail to be adopted.

An important aspect of planning is helping people develop a deeper understanding and appreciation of one another and their differing giftedness. Participants believed that governing boards needed to move toward becoming a covenant community where the members of the board make specific agreements with one another about how they will work together and adhere to those agreements. Participants emphasized the need for quality spiritual formation programs, including the preparation for continual turnover among leadership. They also stressed the importance of continually and carefully linking spiritual disciplines with the spiritual traditions of the congregation and denomination. One summed up the feelings of many in the following comment:

> In order to sustain the culture there must be ongoing conversation about why and how these practices are done. The leadership must model them. They need to take precedence over the "real" work of the organization. Spiritual practices are easily lost when time is short and/or some issues seem to need emergency attention.

Respondents also cited the need for more listening and discernment and the importance of continual evaluation, reflection, celebration, and encouragement. Far too often governing board members are recruited to fill positions with promises such as, "It won't take much time, maybe two hours a month." They carry those expectations with them into board service. Participants repeatedly stressed the need to help people understand the importance of their board roles and what is required if they say yes to the invitation to serve.

Joys, Disappointments, and Dreams

The people participating in this work were overwhelmingly committed to the growth and development of others and the emergence of the church as an institution committed to discerning and living out God's invitation in the day to day. Virtually all shared stories of joy. None spoke of organizational growth, building programs, finances, social ministry, or personal accomplishments in this context. The theme, instead, was the joy of seeing people "getting it." To describe that joy, participants used phrases such as

"finding a sense of completeness,"
"feeling a deeper integration of mind and heart,"
"people previously unheard now speaking,"
"experiencing prayer,"
"working with clergy who understand,"
"witnessing others adopt and repeat practices, language, and ideas," and
"when changes stick."

Participants had something special that they had to share, and they sought to do so whenever they could. They reported deep joy when people received the gift they offered and felt deep disappointment when they did not. Participants felt heartbroken and rejected

"when the leadership allows the work that has been done to go untended or they dismantle it,"
over "how quickly people return to the old way of doing things,"
"when discernment becomes a bad word,"
"when groups have too little time to get done what needs to be done,"
"when people see their work as a drag and do not devote the time to an issue that is necessary to fully understand and work through critical issues,"
"when clergy opt for just getting the business done, so few clergy understand,"
when seeing "politics and control [at work] by both liberals and fundamentalists,"
"when congregations choose to go their own way leaving God out," and
"when people confuse the voices of their egos with the voice of the Spirit."

I find it interesting that the joys reported by participants were, for the most part, rooted in personal relationships; and the disappointments in the way people worked when they gathered to do the business of the church.

The dreams reported by participants of what might emerge from the introduction of spiritual practices into church governing boards focused heavily on the church as institution. They dreamt of

"institutional life becoming more life giving;"

"more leaders understanding the value of facing major issues in a different way;"

"denominations moving from seeking operational managers to spiritual leaders;"

"the time when we will all be open to God, to recognize Christ as the living head and become a church that takes pleasure in seeking God's guidance;" and

"seeing the culture of communities of faith change through the training of pastoral leadership."

Amid the dreams for the institution, participants also talked about some personal dreams for developing specific ministries and being more effective in discerning and following what some participants believed to be their own unattended personal callings.

Spiritual Struggle

The desire to introduce spiritual practices into church governance often appeared to mirror a participant's yearning for a deeper relationship with God personally and corporately. Participants struggled with the difference between what they perceived to be a secular governance model and the more spiritual approach they yearned for. Participants had difficulty with governance models that emphasized dominance, control, and majority rule and that focused on the material dimensions of the church. They questioned their own spiritual practices and described their personal battles with frustration, dryness, and disappointment. They were disappointed with congregational and denominational leaders who seemed bound to the tyranny of the system without ever questioning it or even looking for a better way. Participants typically labored within a context they viewed as largely blind to the Spirit and in which they and others like them felt suffocated. They were compelled by their sense of call, compassion, and a belief that the church can be more life giving. They were frustrated by the continued emphasis on the church's institutional dimensions. Some had at one time or another been seduced by the lure of success in church roles, budgets, attendance, buildings, and programs.

Their desire to introduce spiritual practices into church governance was not some idealistic goal, but a deep yearning for something more than what they had experienced in years of faithful service. Some had continued to work, within their church body, striving to bring changes to that culture. Some had found another call in small groups, new churches, and dying churches—places where the people were willing to see anew because nothing else seemed to work. Some had grown tired and simply stepped away from their previous leadership roles within the institution to focus on one-on-one care and healing. Taken together, their stories offered insight into a critical tension in mainline denominational life. Is the church primarily an institution seeking to survive and thrive, or is the church the body of Christ seeking to discern and live out its call? Is it both and even more? Participants clearly desired to minimize the fighting that seems to characterize church and denominational groups struggling for control in the name of piety, purity, coping with change, or personal preference. Participants sensed a lack of spiritual maturity within the church and yearned for a church that deeply desired to center its attention on listening to God.

Men and Spirituality

Lying just beneath the surface in many comments referenced in this study was the issue of men and spirituality. Something in the language and imagery associated with spirituality appears to elicit a cautious response in many men. I felt this long before I could begin to describe it. The first time I sensed it was during a roundtable on church leadership in the early 1990s. Most of the small group of clergy and lay leaders present were men who held various denominational roles. They were well respected, thoughtful, compassionate, and committed to mission and ministry. Among the women present were several prominent leadership consultants from the business world and not associated with the denomination. They were part of the vanguard opening business to a more spiritual understanding of leadership. As the event unfolded, the tension between their relational, spirit-oriented speech and the more rational, business, religious speech of men present became palpable. The more the women used spiritual and relational language, the more uncomfortable the men appeared to become. It became obvious that the men and women in the room were speaking two different languages and that the men were resistant to what they were hearing.

Why were the men resistant? Part of the resistance no doubt came from this denomination's long and difficult history with the charismatic movement and its traditional mistrust of Christian mysticism. Faith was believed to be a product of reason, not emotion. But I suspect there was more. In *Spirituality for Ministry*, Urban Holmes notes that his research led him to the conclusion that spiritually mature men exhibit a more androgynous personality than the general population.[6] The people he interviewed for his study mirrored the qualities of grace and gentleness that I have observed in the people participating in this study. Holmes also noted a great deal of uneasiness in men with sexuality and the effect sexuality has on spirituality. Brian Pearson, an Anglican priest interested in the midlife transitions in men's lives, talks about the difficulty men in general have with spirituality.[7] He suggests that what men tend to resist is not spiritual practices but the more feminine language and images associated with spirituality. He believes men are prepared to incorporate spiritual practices into their lives if careful attention is given to what the practices are called and how they are discussed. Pearson's experience suggests that the language used to talk about spirituality and governance is extremely important in the male-dominated church world.

When I look at the men and women I know who model the spiritual life in organizations for me (including the people who participated in this study), I am struck by the kindliness, calmness, and willingness to listen they continually model. They do not typically speak of tasks accomplished, projects developed, conflicts won, or other feats of leadership that mark so many conversations in the church governance and administrative arena. They radiate a groundedness in God born in continued reflections into their solitary struggles, the costs of caring about others and the world in which they live, the death of their ambition and ego, and the peace that comes from holding life much more lightly. They have faced the challenges life has presented and learned that personal survival or success is not the point. I am deeply grateful for the men and women who modeled these qualities for me. Such grace and gentleness, however, are not always comfortable for men (and women) who are used to the edgier side of business and government. Their preference is to get in and get on with it. Many seem to view confrontations as the price of progress. My experience suggests that men who are able to share their stories on occasional retreats often find it difficult to be more open in their day-to-day lives. My point, and I believe one shared by many of the participants in this study, is that gender and the language and imagery used to talk about spiritual practices are important and must be accommodated in any serious effort to introduce discernment and prayer into church boards.

Contemporary Movements

Participants reported a wide variety of efforts to introduce spiritual practices into church governance across the contemporary denominational landscape. The picture, as they described it, reminds me of a sea of dandelions popping up all over in an untended lawn. The heavy feet of the institution grounded in business practices, parliamentary procedure, a view of ministry focused on the organization, and conservative versus liberal struggles for power quickly trample many of the efforts, while the climate of self-interest, resistance to change, and desire for control stifles others. It's a tough environment. The participants in this research expressed their feelings of discouragement with the polarization between liberals and conservatives in their denominations. They challenged both those who have laid claim to the rightness of their version of biblical truth and those who seem to place the Scriptures on the back burner in favor of other agendas. They believed too much emphasis is placed on the physical needs of the institution and the "duty" to do what authority figures told them they "should" do. They chafed at what one participant referred to as the "straitjackets of patriarchal culture." At the same time they believed with all their heart that the Spirit was working "under the radar" to bring new life rooted in a deepening desire to listen to God together.

Two of the nine questions I posed to the participants whom I surveyed after the Nashville event asked where they saw signs of encouragement; as they looked for people receptive to introducing spiritual practices in the contemporary church landscape, where did they see hopeful signs? Some reported none; others listed a number of promising future movements or successes in existing congregations or denominational settings. They pointed to a wide array of promising efforts found in diverse groups in mainline Protestant churches, judicatories, and denominations; Roman Catholic parishes; independent evangelical churches; international ecumenical church organizations; classrooms; religious communities; spiritually oriented nonprofits; and parachurch groups. They also cited signs of longing for something more in both for-profit and not-for-profit sectors, which I have already referred to in other chapters. It seems that wherever people hunger to better understand the will of God, or simply long for wholeness and meaning in work, and recognize that there can be something more, there is life.

Another Perspective

Several participants who provided written responses to my nine questions believed the spiritual practices I used as examples for my survey (reflection, prayer, storytelling, biblical and theological reflection, silence, yielding, visioning, and evaluating) were too narrow. They rightly reasoned, as Urban Holmes's spirituality model illustrates, that spiritual practices are not limited to the more contemplative ones I had listed. One person said,

> I do all this [consulting work with congregations] because in my gut I think *everything* we are doing is spiritual practice. Discussing "screwups" the congregation experienced? We're working on confession and absolution. Discussing budget problems? We are grappling with the incarnation of the community—the "flesh" on the "body." Talking about how the community has changed? We're on the edge of prophetic discernment. Worrying about the lack of volunteers and leaders? We're talking about what it means to be called and to call others. Trying to figure out a plan for the next decade? We're asking what God is calling the congregation to become.

The person continued,

> What I do is hard-nosed design. I try to figure out where they are and what will help them move on from there. I don't have a list of spiritual practices I plan to use. I have all sorts of thoughts and designs to help them locate themselves, develop deeper relationships with each other, and find out where they need to be going.

The mistake I made when I first tried to introduce discernment into a governing board, and I suspect the one that many others have also made, was that I was still too focused on figuring out what was going on, building relationships, and helping the organization move toward its goals. It was a formula for failure. Tools and practitioners must match. People whose temperament, experience, and skills have been honed in the bureaucratic structures of the church will likely be uncomfortable with a discernment process and may not see ways in which it can be used, especially to address emotional issues in which positions are well established. The continuing challenge is to use both the gifts that help governing boards develop the capacity to listen and those that enable them to more effectively act. One participant noted that church organizations have the opportunity to draw the best from both the world of the business and parliamentary process and the world of spiritual disciplines. "I hope the church can realize the awesome gift we have as a 'business' able to use spiritual practices to guide and direct our decision making."

I hope so, too. We in the church need to recognize the value of diverse gifts such as the spiritual practices we have inherited through the church, the learnings from contemporary business that enable us to better manage and lead organizations, and the revelations about the nature of the creation emerging from science. If we do, the church can begin to offer new models of leadership and organizational behavior to the vast array of institutions that contemporary societies depend on. Such models can help us be more faithful and effective stewards of the gospel we have been entrusted with and do a better job of caring for God's creation.

Change

Intentionally listening to God brings change. People change, and our governing boards change. One participant in the Nashville gathering told the group, "We lost people. I changed my leadership style. I was no longer the vision-casting leader. I learned to wait, to not know. I found it unsettling and risky. It is good to be shaped by Christ, but it costs something." One respondent to my nine questions wrote, "As we continue in spiritual practice, we are beckoned out beyond our habitual comfort zones into the refiner's fire of our ongoing conversion and repentance so that . . . we grow to see as God sees." We do not remain who we were when we set out to more intentionally listen to God. We change, often in ways we are unprepared for. When I was desperate to find a way to counter the contentious climate and absence of focus in the congregational governing board I was chairing, I began to look around for help. Armed with the vision of a more spiritual board I had gathered from a workshop on storytelling, conducted by Worshipful-Work founder Chuck Olsen, and a few new tools I had collected along the way from the business world, I set out to change *my* board.

The board made some significant strides, but not because we practiced corporate spiritual discernment, at least as I understand it now. We changed because people began to listen to one another and, I think, personally to God, but the process did not quite look or feel like I had hoped. I tried reading, but the books I found were either by mystics whose writings I could not connect to governance or by evangelical leaders who seemed primarily focused (as I had been) on creating large corporate structures designed to harvest souls and provide aid to the poor. I felt a need for something more in church governance, but I could not find either the resources or the mentors to help me understand my yearning. In doing this research I learned that there are many people like me who yearn for a governing climate that attends first to listening to God and who feel isolated and alone.

My eight years on Worshipful-Work's governing board proved to be the turning point, because it put me in contact with others who believe that listening to God together ought to be the first priority of governance. Because changing church governance involves both one's own and the governing board's spiritual walk, the process is slow and often difficult. Many of the participants spoke of intense personal struggles with starting or sustaining their own spiritual practices. They talked about their frustrations, dryness, and disappointment. One person shared, "My own spiritual life was suffering from the dissonance of trying to live as God's person within an organization that was living according to the worst of the world's dysfunctions. It was as much to save my own life as it was to serve my organization that I sought to lead it toward Worshipful Work." They contended with congregational and denominational leaders who appeared to be bound to the tyranny of the existing system. Another expressed the frustration of many: "In addition, I've found resistance to the claims of the Gospel by those who occupy seats of authority and power in the judicatories of my church, and even hostility to attempts to implement them. While this is not surprising, it has been very disheartening and discouraging." Participants struggle with the idea that the governance model most commonly used within the church emphasizes dominance, control, and majority rule and focuses on the material matters of the church. One person said, "After crying for a day, I actually felt an enormous sense of deliverance. (Yes, that's the word.) Almost like, 'Let the institution go. The present form needs to die. Go where I send you and leave the rest up to me.'" Participants in general shared the compelling belief that the church could be so much more than it was, and they yearned for the fresh air of change.

Our Shadow Side

As we change, we frequently find ourselves confronted with things about ourselves that we have denied, repressed, or neglected in order to maintain a more idealized image of what we would like to be. One of the participants who had experienced some success in introducing spiritual practices into a parachurch organization cautioned me that it will force people to confront their shadow side. Richard Rohr reminds his readers in *Everything Belongs* that we need to pay attention to "what we dismiss and what we disdain. Look at what we've spent our whole life avoiding."[8] The same person who spoke of confronting one's shadow side also pointed out, "As grace begins its long slow work in us, shadow pieces of our lives are revealed much the same way the unclean spirits were outed by Jesus's presence." Multiply the shadow pieces of each board member's life by the number of board members plus the number of other people who are directly affected by the introduction of spiritual practices and you have the potential for a lot of personal and relational change. Changes in the pattern of human relationships will be uncomfortable for some, perhaps many. This participant cautioned that there would be people within your congregation or organization who simply don't want to deal with their personal shadow side or that of their organization. Some will say, "Forget it," and withdraw; others will overtly resist. Those who continue with the organization will do so as changed people, people who have "been purified and strengthened" by this confrontation with their shadow and who will "bring the gifts that emerge back into world and community. We go as people of a different realm into a world that does not speak the same language, and . . . 'bearing the social cost of our conversion.'"

Spiritual practices don't influence God's love. Instead, they foster a deeper awareness of God within us, and they help us gain a greater level of self-understanding, perceive the needs and yearnings of others, and hear the cries of our world. Spiritual practices help us to hear God. As we hear God, we change. And as we change, we begin to see God and the people and organizations that fill our lives in a different light. As our perceptions change, we are forced to see ourselves in new ways and revisit past thoughts and experiences in new ways. This new way of seeing has a social cost, as the participant quoted above observes. When I began to intentionally focus my life around silence, biblical and theological reflection, intercessory prayer, service, and discernment, I found myself increasingly estranged from some beliefs, activities, and relationships that had been central to my life and drawn toward others. I felt the need to say no to many activities in my congregation and denomination where I had previously said yes, and those choices brought changes. My transition has not always been easy to explain or to live out, but it has been, as I have learned, a necessary one.

Practical Wisdom

The people who responded to my nine questions and those who gathered in Nashville had a great deal of practical wisdom to share, wisdom I wish I would have had access to at an earlier point in my church career. Virtually all emphasized the importance of spiritual companionship that enables one to talk about his or her personal spiritual journey as well as the issues arising from introducing spiritual practices into the organization. They pointed out that if you are the pastor or the chair of the governing board, you may be able to introduce spiritual practices, but you will also need others to own the goal to make listening to God together the central feature of your governing culture. They emphasized the need for the pastor or board chair to talk to the governing board about their experiences and yearnings and to engage the board in conversation about how they might listen to God together. They cautioned against announcing that you had discovered a better way of doing the church's business and then proceeding to implement *your* ideas. Introducing spiritual practices into governance is a fundamental shift for most church organizations, and a board needs to be fully involved in the whole process from the beginning. Participants warned that your vision of a governing board committed to corporate spiritual practices may not be accepted, but encouraged patience and persistence. They cautioned that you cannot force your board to adopt spiritual practices, so don't try.

Those leading such a change will need spiritual companionship and mentoring all along the way. Participants emphasized the need to seek out others both within your organization and outside of it who share your passion and desire, and draw them in. Some pointed out the need to look beyond your own faith tradition for insights. They reasoned that leadership, organizational life, and spiritual practices transcend the boundaries we in the church erect within and around ourselves, so don't be afraid to search for success among others and learn from them. Participants emphasized the importance of a faithful community who will listen and pray with you and gather together regularly to do so. Go slowly and build well, they suggested; most efforts to introduce spiritual practices fail because people try to rush the process.

There are many more resources available to help church leaders introduce spiritual practices than when I began looking in the mid-1990s. The bibliography in this book contains a list of resources that have been helpful to me and to others. Treat them as learning tools, however, not road maps. You cannot take someone else's idea or model of discernment and simply run with it. You have to make it your own, and this means you will be continually inventing and reinventing most of what you do as you go. Remember, developing the communal capacity to listen to God is the most important thing you will do together as a governing board.

Participants recommended that if you choose to try to incorporate spiritual discernment in your governing board, work with less controversial issues first so that you can develop the skill and trust necessary to address larger, more contentious issues. They believed you should allow people to experience success, and carefully evaluate what works and what does not. Every experience is a learning opportunity, even when the effort appears to have failed. Participants suggested that you seek to learn from those who resist including spiritual practices in your governing board. Emphasize that spiritual practices are not simply another technique to make better decisions in your organization; they are essential life skills. The people participating in this research continually cautioned against telling people what to do, even if you know. Tell them what you see, hear, and feel, and invite them to experience it. They emphasized that you are making an offering when you share with others on your board what you are experiencing. They have an offering to make, too, so do it together.

Good spiritual mentoring is important. The need for a spiritual director was a consistent theme among participants. Spiritual directors, spiritual centers, seminaries, and retreat centers are scattered all across the country; use them. Since most people have not attempted to introduce spiritual practices to their organizations before, participants in this study recommended that anyone considering this step seek out guides who have experience in the process. Several participants also recommended including someone from outside the organization in the governing board meetings to help the board more objectively listen and reflect on what it is doing and consider whether that is consistent with the goal of listening more attentively to God together. Participants also felt it was important to continually link the spiritual practices they were advocating to the historic piety and spirituality within the congregational and denominational traditions and the biblical narrative. They believed that the continuing connection helped people build important bridges between the spiritual practices being introduced and their past faith experiences. They consistently recommended that anyone trying to introduce spiritual practices should help people relax with the practices they sought to introduce so that others would be less inclined to see those spiritual practices as potential instruments of manipulation. While there will always be people who view any change in governing practices as manipulation, the potential can be reduced by establishing a test period during which you try communal discernment on a particular issue, let people experience the process, evaluate the experience, incorporate the learnings, and try again.

Another consistent theme among participants was that congregational leaders should remember good things take time. Be persistent, be consistent, be patient, work slowly, and don't give up. Participants stressed the need to empathize with the struggles of others who may not see in the spiritual practices the value that you do. Encourage a climate of continued experimentation to determine how the practices will work best. The desire for control, predictability, conformity, security, and minimal risk within church governing boards is strong. Participants continually emphasized the need to take time and listen for the God's leadings. They emphasized the need to help people see God's presence in all things, to help them acquire the vocabulary they need to express their feelings and what they are experiencing, and to allow them time to become comfortable with spiritual practices. The need to be sensitive to the anxiety change brings, to continually attend to the emotional issues associated with transition, and to remember that you cannot practice discernment together if you do not live it in your personal lives were themes repeatedly stressed by participants.

Concluding Thoughts

At the close of the Nashville collegium, Loretta Ross, a Presbyterian pastor, author, and executive director of the Sanctuary Foundation for Prayer, who also served as a listener for the event, summarized what she heard. The questions Loretta heard the people in Nashville asking themselves offer another perspective of the complexity of board life that is revealed when people commit themselves to listen more deeply to one another with the heart rather than with the head. I felt her observations were especially insightful. I know I have quietly asked each of them many times when I have joined a new group. The following are the questions Loretta heard participants asking:

- Who are the other people with me here at this gathering?
- Who am I in this context?
- Where am I encountering God here?
- Is this place safe?
- Will I belong?
- Will my gift, my voice, and my offering be received?
- Is there space here for me to be me?
- What needs to happen here for us to belong to one another?
- What difference will this make to the poorest person in the world?
- What summons, calls out the need for discernment?

I wonder what church governance would look like if boards took the time to honor such questions. Would we grind to a halt, as many believe, or might we discover a new way of being together? I suspect the participants in this research believe that if we truly listened to one another and to God together, we might indeed discover a new way of governance. Ross concluded her reflections on the collegium with a question to God, "What do you require of us to hear your Word to us?" What she heard from God in response was: People need to feel and be safe, utterly safe, free from judgment and criticism; they need to know they are loved deeply and cherished; and they need to be purified of internal impediments—to have their vision cleansed and made right and righteous, reconciled and trued to the ordering principles of God's creation.

Most participants in this study have felt isolated at various times because of their yearnings to focus on listening to God together and their often frustrating attempts to integrate spiritual practices into governing board life. Yet they believe they are part of a groundswell of interest that is springing up all over. One of the Nashville collegium participants observed, "It is a revolution. It is popping up in very unexpected places. God says, 'Wait. Hold on.'" In their view, God is in the midst of doing a new thing (Isa. 43:19). Is becoming a listening community an unrealistic dream for a few starry-eyed spiritual optimists who can't deal with the realities of institutional life, or a real possibility if we simply seek to listen to God together?

Certainly a number of people across the church are trying to incorporate spiritual practices into church governance and specifically to practice corporate discernment, but the practices, however important, are not the goal. The people participating in the Nashville collegium continually emphasized that the practice of discernment was not a magic bullet. One Nashville participant captured the essence of people's feelings: "I'm not in love with discernment. I am in love with the God who speaks to us." The participants at the Nashville collegium stressed that each of us needs to take off our institutional glasses if we are to truly hear the God who speaks to us. Grounding our lives in listening to God is, unfortunately, new for many church governing boards. Participants emphasized, "You can't go someplace new with the directions to somewhere else," and the directions most of us have are ones for running a business or government. Those directions allow us to manage activities and adjudicate differences within the institution but do little to equip us to listen to God together. The people who participated in this study have tried to break free of the institutional imagination that so shapes the way church is done and to reimagine how congregations, denominations, and other church organizations might work if they focused their intentions on listening to God together.

6

Imagination

CARLO CARRETTO WAS A TWENTIETH-CENTURY ROMAN Catholic lay teacher whose writings have become a guide for many. Carretto sought to walk in the footsteps of Jesus. That journey took him from a life in the institutional church, into the North African desert, then back again into society. He became convinced that contemplation and action were inextricably connected. In his letters to his sister, published in *Letters to Dolcidia: 1954–1983*, he writes,

> You see, I've done a lot of work for the Church—I'm aware of it. It has been my only thought, my only care. I have raced hard and covered as many miles as the most committed missionary. At a certain point it occurred to me that what the church lacked was not work, activity, the building of projects or the commitment to bring in souls. What was missing, *or at least was scarce, was the element of prayer, meditation, self-giving, intimacy with God, fidelity to the Holy Spirit and the conviction that [Christ] was the real builder of the Church*: in a word, the supernatural element. Let me make myself clear: people of action are needed in the Church but we have to be very careful that their action *does not smother the more delicate but much more important element of prayer*. If action is missing and there is prayer, the Church lives on, it keeps on breathing, but if prayer is missing and there is only action, the Church withers and dies (italics added).[1]

In what ways might "the element of prayer, meditation, self-giving, intimacy with God, fidelity to the Holy Spirit and the conviction that

[Christ] was the real builder of the Church" identified by Carretto be more fully integrated into the governance and administration of today's church? The answer lies in reimaging these critical functions and the leadership the church relies on to guide them.

Context

To fully understand why the church governs itself the way it does, we have to keep the culture that surrounds and permeates the church in full view. As pointed out in chapter 1, the church is both subtly and profoundly shaped by Western culture. Over the past century, institutions, especially large corporate entities set up to offer products and services at a profit to their owners, have come to dominate North American society. People depend on these institutions for virtually everything, including the resources and services we need to sustain life, employment, security, education, the arts, and opportunities to develop our talents. These entities have a tremendous potential rooted in the talent, creativity, resources, and capacity for service at their disposal as well as a dehumanizing and exploitive dimension that emerges when owners and managers pursue self-centered short-term interests. Many recognize the destructive and dehumanizing effects of corporate power and self-interest. As a result, a movement toward a greater wholeness and openness to the spiritual dimensions of our lives within institutions is evident. The voices seeking greater openness to the spirit within the corporate community are not always Christian, however. Many (possibly most) are rooted in the richness of Eastern or Native American traditions, which are less obsessed with time, private ownership, and personal gain. While Christianity has long understood the need for stillness and silence, that God is the owner of all things, and that people are called to be stewards of God's creation, the importance of these principles is often eclipsed by our emphasis in Western society on action, rational thinking, and economic value.

Karen Armstrong, a former Roman Catholic nun who has written extensively in the field of comparative religions, believes Westerners have allowed our imaginations to be shaped by what we are capable of knowing and describing in a rational way. As a result, spirituality has been marginalized in favor of theology, experience in favor of knowledge, the mystical in favor of the revealed, and the servant in favor of the hierarchy. Among the people I studied, their desire to incorporate spiritual practices into the church's governance and administrative structures stems from their dissatisfaction and disillusionment with the existing system and the deep desire to become more attentive to God. Greater attentiveness, in the eyes of most authors and participants in my survey, requires a greater emphasis on prayer (especially listening prayer), a climate of respect and trust, a commitment to learning, the practice of corporate biblical and theological reflection, the capacity for collective spiritual discernment, and more emphasis on spiritual formation of clergy and laypeople. It is a tall order by any measure, but it is a goal worthy of the quest.

Episcopalian theology professors Owen Thomas and Ellen Wondra write in their *Introduction to Theology* that the fact the church was founded by the Holy Spirit has often been forgotten because "it brings into the picture a revolutionary freedom that is viewed somewhat uneasily by those concerned with proper form, order, and continuity."[2] We have over the centuries, especially within Protestantism, consistently placed a higher value on rational thinking than other ways of knowing. Can the church now address its own uneasiness with what is spiritual and the tension between spirituality and administration? The challenges are formidable, but the need to try persists. The people who participated in Worshipful-Work events faced such challenges in the congregations and organizations they served. Sometimes they have seen spiritual practices incorporated into church governance; often they have not.

Ideas about how people organize and govern ourselves are always based on implicit images that persuade us to see, understand, and manage situations in a particular way. The images we hold of organization and leadership are especially powerful. They determine the ways we work together to address the challenges we face. Most people have great difficulty getting beyond the hierarchical images of *organization* and *leadership* and the assumptions we make about them. In many church bodies the associated images and language about how we should organize and lead are so sacred that people find it difficult to accept even the suggestion of imagining things any other way. The church's challenge is to recognize the power of the leadership and organization images we hold—the extent to which they shape what we view as possible and blind us to other potential. In short, our imaginations define our world. The question is, Are our imaginations adequate for us to meet the challenges of the future? Or, to paraphrase Anglican clergyman and writer J. B. Phillips, are they too small?[3]

Perhaps the first question we need to ask ourselves is how do we imagine the church? Our imagination of what church governance can be is shaped by the images we hold of church. Avery Dulles, scholar, teacher, theologian, and a member of the College of Cardinals in the Roman Catholic Church, believes the church can be seen in five ways—as an institution, a herald, a mystical communion, a sacrament, and a servant. Each congregation or other church organization typically embraces some aspect of each of the five models all the time but tends to emphasize one or more in response to outside pressures and interior movement.

The institutional model, as described by Dulles, is the visible church. It consists of the organization, leadership, and authority structures; formally approved doctrines; sacraments; duly appointed pastors; and buildings. The herald model emphasizes the proclamation of the gospel and conversion. Church organizations included in the herald model are typically independent of one another but bound together through their common response to the gospel, in contrast to the institutional model, which is more typically associated with denominations that include regional, national, and international hierarchies. Both the institutional and the herald models are practical models that place a great deal of emphasis on authority, structure, organized activity, and visible association with the organization.

But the church, as we well know, is more than the tangible aspects of organization and mission. The church is also a mystical communion, an organic community that transcends physical description, people gathered in God who carry the graces and gifts of the Holy Spirit. The church is also sacramental, the community of the baptized who gather around the table of Christ to take part in the Eucharist. The goal of the church, according to this model, is to purify and intensify people's response to the grace of Christ. In each of these four models, according to Dulles, the church is the subject and the world the object that the church acts upon or seeks to influence. The fifth model, the servant, envisions the church as a community of disciples serving the world. This model emphasizes believing people helping others regardless of church affiliation. The desire of the servant model is that all people around the world might hear the gospel, participate in the sacraments, receive comfort and encouragement, experience a respectful hearing of their deepest longings, and find the material help they need to thrive. Dulles believes the church can ultimately and only be understood as mystery. But while the church may be mystery, it is also tangible. People must be able to think about it, live with it, work in it, talk about it, point toward it, and continue to be both stewards of it and servants to it. A useful image of the church must therefore embrace mystery and revelation, organization and organism, spirit and model, human and divine. The image must be large enough to point toward the rich diversity of human experience and the ways that God speaks to all humanity (some would say creation) and small enough to be wherever people of God gather.[4]

Limited Imagination

I believe the real challenge the church faces in listening to God together is our limited capacity to imagine. We are so invested in our ways of doing business in the organized church that we frequently cannot see beyond them. The fundamental critique of participants in the July 2006 Nashville collegium, the people who responded to my nine-question survey, and many of the authors whose works have influenced my thinking over the years is that the images we hold of organization life, leadership, and the capacity of people to do the work before them limit our ability to be better stewards of the gospel and our world. The attempt to integrate spiritual practices into church governance or to introduce spirituality into the business community and public education simply calls the limits of our capacity to imagine to the forefront.

Before venturing further, I need to say a few words about imagination. First, imagination is not the same as fantasy or make-believe. Fantasy is not tied to reality; imagination is. Imagination is built on the facts, truths, and realities of life. Imagination is our capacity to see those facts, truths, and realities with new eyes and to reframe our circumstances in ways that draw forth new insights and meaning. Imagination allows us to keep our whole life connected even if we cannot make all fit rationally. Our imaginations allow us to move beyond the circumstances in which we live—to dream about a better way of being together, doing things differently, or becoming something more than what we are. Too many of us lose the capacity to imagine during our childhood. An educator friend of mine believes that within the first few grades of elementary school, children's capacity to associate diverse elements that defy logical connection is systematically reduced by a formal education process that emphasizes rational thought and by societal pressures to conform. Perhaps it was young children's capacity to freely associate that Jesus had in mind when he told the adults standing around him that they needed to become like little children.

To imagine is to escape the chains that restrict the way we think; it is a gift that must continually be nurtured through association with other creative people. Urban Holmes equates imagination with the capacity to engage the full brain (and by extension the full community) in the process of discerning, developing, and deciding. He contrasts imagination to our focus on the rational. People are not just creatures who think logically and analytically; they also intuit and associate in ways that cannot be described but only experienced. This capacity for wholeness is the context in which God's self-disclosure and revelation occur. Imagination enables us to truly see beyond the phenomena that confront us to the underlying meaning of what we are encountering. But while our imaginations help us see some things clearly, they can also blind us. The images and metaphors that enlist our imaginations to create powerful new insights often leave us struggling to grasp others. To the extent this happens, we become trapped in our imaginations.

Such is often the case with issues surrounding organization and leadership. We become trapped in ways of organizing and leading that result from assumptions such as people are unmotivated or incapable of performing the work that needs to be done, or as is often the case in church, people are simply not permitted by God to do it. The result is a constant pressure on people to reduce their lives and their imagination of what life can be to that found within prescribed roles. Today a great conversation is going on across our society about life within organizations, how that life should be structured, the capacity and motivation of people, and what the leadership should be. Increasing numbers of people seem to be imagining more collegial ways of people working together that place less emphasis on traditional top-down authority structures and more emphasis on developing the diverse gifts and talents people possess. Many imagine organizations less concerned with the institution's survival and prosperity and more concerned with the needs of people and the care of creation. This conversation extends beyond conventional categories of conservative versus liberal, fundamentalist versus New Age, Eastern versus Western, industrial versus postindustrial, religious versus secular, socialist versus capitalist, pro-life versus pro-choice, and the host of other broad-brush attempts we make to differentiate, label, and often demonize each other. The issue of introducing spiritual practices into church governance rests in the midst of this larger struggle over how to imagine organizations and leadership.

People use various language to attempt to describe what they believe is wrong with the way human activity is organized and leadership is defined and what needs to be done to change it. Margaret Wheatley, an early influence in the metamorphosis of my imagination, whom I referenced earlier, uses the terms *old story* and *new story*.[5] According to Wheatley, the old story is one of power and control. Until the late twentieth century, the old story was reinforced by science's earlier view of the world as an ordered universe of discrete particles and forces whose behavior was knowable, predictable, and to that extent controllable. These ideas about a completely rational world have captivated Western thought and helped to create a culture that presumes human activity can be organized and managed as if people function like parts of a machine. This old story still dominates many of our imaginations about how to organize and lead. The new story is rooted in a very different set of assumptions about human capacity and motivation. It emphasizes relationships, uniqueness, free will, and creativity found in the new sciences and many native cultures. Wheatley asks her readers to set aside their machinelike imaginations and to view organizations as living systems where there is no such thing as an independent individual and no need for leaders to assume the responsibilities they have demanded in the past.

Author, organizational consultant, and social activist Peter Block is another person who has helped people around the world begin to reimagine leadership and organizations. Like Wheatley, Block is critical of old-story imagination, which he terms *patriarchy*. He believes that our emphasis on strong, male leadership; predictability; and control has produced a culture of dependency instead of encouraging people to develop their own capacity. He asserts, "To state it bluntly strong leadership does not have within itself the capability to create the fundamental changes our organizations require. It is not the fault of the people in these positions, it is the fault of the way we have framed the role. The effect is to localize power, purpose, and privilege in the one we call leader."[6] Like Wheatley, Block believes our overemphasis on models of leadership and organization that stress strong, centralized male leadership limits our ability to address contemporary society's challenges. He imagines instead a system where responsibility and control are decoupled and where partnership, empowerment, and service are key values. Unfortunately, the continued use of terms such as *leadership*, *organization*, *authority*, and *responsibility* paralyzes our imagination. Block's alternative term is *stewardship*, which means serving and being accountable without needing to be in control.

Social scientist and attorney Riane Eisler uses the words *domination* and *partnership* to frame the contrasting models of organizations and leadership she sees in society. Like Wheatley and Block, she too is critical of the existing system for its emphasis on power and its corrosive influence on human community and development. She writes, "In the domination model somebody has to be on top and somebody has to be on the bottom. Those on top control those below them. People learn, starting in early childhood, to obey orders without question. They learn to carry a harsh voice in their heads telling them they're no good, they don't deserve love, they need to be punished. Families and societies are based on control that is explicitly or implicitly backed up by guilt, fear, and force. The world is divided into in-groups and out-groups, with those who are different seen as enemies to be conquered or destroyed."[7] Her partnership model, in contrast, supports mutually respectful and caring relationships. She believes a partnership perspective frees individuals, families, and whole societies to grow mentally, emotionally, and spiritually in ways that hierarchies cannot. Eisler thinks that imagining our life together through the partnership lens encourages greater joy and playfulness among people, increases our opportunity to learn and to be creative, and shifts the exercise of power to empower rather than disempower others.

The contrasting images of organizational life and leadership offered by Wheatley, Block, and Eisler are typical of the authors whose works I have read and the responses from participants in my research. There are many others. Before I stopped counting, I recorded fifty-eight contrasting word pairs, some of which are included in table 1. The column labeled "Existing Organizational Cultures" contains those qualities people generally ascribe to current organization culture.

TABLE 1. EXISTING AND LONGED-FOR STYLES OF ORGANIZATION

EXISTING ORGANIZATIONAL CULTURES	LONGED-FOR ORGANIZATIONAL CULTURES
Hierarchy, top-down	Servant, bottom-up
Authority	Giftedness
Expert training	Self-directed learning
Competitive	Cooperative
Scarcity	Abundance
Motivated by financial considerations and desire to build a sustainable identity	Motivated by people's needs and the development of relevant community
Doing	Being
Tangible	Transcendent
Task focused	Relationship focused
Pathology	Emergence
Domination	Actualization
Religion	Spirituality
White, male dominated	Egalitarian
Facts	Story
Consistency and predictability	Mystery
Consumption	Development
Military and sports metaphors	Organic relational metaphors
Knowing	Learning
Answer	Question

These cultures emphasize things that are more tangible, definable, logical, predictable, and controllable. The "Longed-For Organizational Cultures" column describes an opposing pole where greater value is placed on listening, giftedness, collaboration, flexibility, and creativity. The qualities listed in "Longed-For" column have typically been pushed aside in Western culture in favor of those listed in the "Existing" column. The result is that people whose views more naturally align with the "Longed-For" column are less likely to have a voice in governance and administration in our society's institutions, including the church.

A Christian Contrast

So far, I have been talking primarily about the imaginations that shape the way we organize and govern across our society. What about our imaginations as Christian people? I first read Walter Brueggemann's book *The Prophetic Imagination* during my service as a church executive. I soon found myself reflecting on how deeply my imagination of the church and its governance conformed to what Brueggemann defines as *the royal imagination*. The royal imagination is schooled in the governing and administrative mindset of the institution. Its goal is to preserve the organization and grow its influence. It is the type of imagination that the Old Testament kings (and those associated with the royal court and the temple) would likely have had, and all too prevalent in the church today. The royal imagination sees the world through the eyes of someone responsible for maintaining and developing what exists. The prophetic imagination, on the other hand, sees the world through the eyes of those without power, those outside the organization. It is focused on the injustices perpetrated by the organization and on the plight of the powerless. The prophet and the king see the world very differently. Their visions of the future, their understanding of possibilities, and the choices they are likely to make result from two distinctly different imaginations. The dichotomy presented is a classic case of the insider versus the outsider, of people in power versus people without power. When I read Brueggemann's book I was an insider and had been one all my life. I didn't know what it was not to have a voice in how "the system" worked. My energy and creativity were directed toward maintaining the organization, and my royal imagination essentially blinded me to the needs of the poor and the environment. As I look back, I can point to people who had prophetic voices, but regrettably I (and those around me) viewed them more as nuisances, because they disrupted the *royal* work we focused on.

The Gospel writers frame this great fissure dividing people's imagination about organization and governance in terms of *ruler* or *master* versus *servant*. Matthew records the following response to James and John's mother's request for her sons to be seated in positions of privilege in Jesus's kingdom: "Jesus called them together and said, 'You know that the rulers of the Gentiles lord it over them, and their high officials exercise authority over them. Not so with you. Instead, whoever wants to become great among you must be your servant, and whoever wants to be first must be your slave—just as the Son of Man did not come to be served, but to serve, and to give his life as a ransom for many'" (Matt. 20:25–28).

The contrast between Jesus's imagination and those of his disciples was so significant that Jesus chose to begin his last evening with the disciples by washing their feet and admonishing them to do likewise (John 13). Still, they apparently failed to grasp the meaning of what Jesus had done, and the topic came up again later in the evening while they reclined at the table. Luke tells the story: "A dispute also arose among them as to which of them was considered to be greatest. Jesus said to them, 'The kings of the Gentiles lord it over them; and those who exercise authority over them call themselves Benefactors. But you are not to be like that. Instead, the greatest among you should be like the youngest, and the one who rules like the one who serves. For who is greater, the one who is at the table or the one who serves? Is it not the one who is at the table? But I am among you as one who serves'" (22:24–27). Jesus's words did not resolve the ruler-servant imagination issue, and it persists throughout the church.

Being a servant while bearing the responsibilities of leadership in an organization is often a challenge because of the contradictory images people hold of a servant and a leader. But if we can allow our imaginations to shift so that we see the role as teacher or guide or even a companion in a learning process, the apparent contradictions between servant and leader disappear. As a servant, one's role is to prepare those who serve to handle greater and greater challenges. Being a servant does not absolve a person in a leadership role from exercising strong and sometimes directive leadership when such is called for; it simply shifts one's imagination about what it means to be a leader. No longer is a leader understood as someone whose role is to control and direct. Rather, a leader's responsibility is to develop the capacity of others to meet the challenges of their continually changing environment. Robert Greenleaf's definition of someone who is both servant and leader was hammered out on the forge of a long career in a large multinational corporation and his reflections as a Quaker on that experience. His definition bears repeating.

> It begins with the natural feeling that one wants to serve, to serve *first*. Then conscious choice brings one to aspire to lead. . . . The difference [between the leader-first and servant-first] manifests itself in the care taken by the servant-first to make sure that other people's highest priority needs are being served. The best test . . . is: Do those served grow as persons? Do they, *while being served*, become healthier, wiser, freer, more autonomous, more likely themselves to become servants? And, what is the effect on the least privileged in society? Will they benefit or at least not be further deprived?[8] (Italics added.)

The New Testament does not resolve the ruler-servant issue. It leaves us with both models. In his book *Ministry in the New Testament*, Yale University professor David Bartlett states his belief that Paul emphasized the more organic and open approach to organizing the church (Rom. 12:4–8; 1 Cor. 12:12–30; Eph. 4:11–16; Col. 2:19) because he saw in that model a greater potential for being open to the Spirit's movement. The authors of the more formal, hierarchical models of the pastoral letters (1 Tim. 3:1–13; 4:13–14; Titus 1:5–16), Bartlett contends, were more influenced by the need to maintain order among groups of people relatively new to the faith. Bartlett concludes that it is not one or the other, but what serves the gospel in a specific context that must be followed, which is exactly what the servant imagination emphasizes. The following story from Richard Foster's book *Prayer* captures Bartlett's point.

Jean Vanier, the founder of the L'Arche communities for mentally handicapped people, often explains with a simple illustration his approach to those who live at L'Arche. He will cup his hands lightly and say, "Suppose I have a wounded bird in my hands. What would happen if I closed my hands completely?" The response is immediate: "Why, the bird will be crushed and die." "Well, then, what would happen if I opened my hands completely?" "Oh, no, then the bird will try to fly away, and it will fall and die." Vanier smiles and says, "The right place is like my cupped hand, neither totally open nor totally closed. It is the space where growth can take place."

For us, too, the hands of God are cupped lightly. We have enough freedom so that we can stretch and grow, but also we have enough protection so that we will not be injured—and so we can be healed. This is the Prayer of Rest.[9]

The mistake I believe many of us make with the descriptions of leadership and organization in the pastoral letters is to make them the end rather than the means to further development. In my view, the dichotomy Bartlett points out and Vanier so artfully illustrates is a form of what contemporary leadership gurus Paul Hersey and Ken Blanchard call *situational leadership*. Briefly, situational leadership says that you do what is necessary to provide the best environment for people to meet the challenges they face and to grow individually and corporately, depending on the context and conditions, the capabilities of the people, and the gifts of the leader. We err when we assume the more structured form is the end, when it should be seen as simply the means to a deeper relationship captured by the servant model given us by Jesus.

This conversation has yet another level that extends beyond the contrasting images of organization life and the apparent paradox of being servant and leader. British cultural anthropologist Victor Turner offers this slant. He uses the terms *antistructure* and *structure* to refer to the types of organizational qualities I list under "Longed-For Organizational Cultures" and "Existing Organizational Cultures" respectively. Urban Holmes, in his book *Ministry and Imagination*, cites Turner in developing his arguments for the importance of imagination in ministry. Holmes points out that structure is essential to the cohesion and sustainability of any society, but so too is the capacity to step outside society, which is what the term *antistructure* refers to. It is the capacity to step outside the structures and conventions of social systems that allows us to see in new ways, to experience life in ways less mediated by the systems around us, and to listen to God and our world outside the din of the day to day. Holmes argues that we cannot allow our structures to define us. Our spiritual and societal health requires that we be able to regularly step beyond our structures to experience more fully the God who transcends them.

He analogizes this rhythm of regularly stepping outside the structure of our day-to-day lives to the rhythm of the Jewish Feast of Booths during harvest season, when the Hebrews moved outside their homes into temporary dwellings to help them reclaim the perspective of their ancestors during their sojourn in the wilderness. Sukkoth, as the Feast of Booths was more properly known, was a time of pilgrimage from the safety and predictability of the community they currently enjoyed back to the time when they lived in the more uncertain conditions of the barren wilderness. Both the structure and the antistructure dimensions of life are essential. The movement between the two is pilgrimage.

This capacity to regularly step outside the day-to-day world of organizational business is the essence of spiritual disciplines practiced as part of church governance, which participants in my research believe is vital. According to Turner, early Protestantism diminished the role of pilgrimage because it appeared to contribute little to saving souls.[10] We err when we think that pilgrimage is wasted time, however. Regular pilgrimage enables us to cultivate a transcendent perspective of our social system, which then allows us to more clearly discern God's invitation. Pilgrimage, as Holmes and Turner use the term, permits us to get beneath the structures of our lives and to experience how it feels to depend on God. When we step outside the security of our structures, we discover a world as different from the everyday world we experience as the chaotic subatomic world is different from the one Newton first described. The movement from structure to antistructure is a movement from a world ordered in predictable and controllable ways to a world ordered in ways that we can only partially describe, from a world filled with regulated social interactions and prescriptions to a place of emptiness and potential.

We can experience pilgrimage in our personal sabbath practices and regular retreats, but we need to be intentional about setting time aside for solitude, listening, and reflection.

Reimagining Organization

What if we could step outside the way we think about organizations; what might we imagine? Imagining other ways of working together is a challenge because the images we consciously and unconsciously hold of organizations are powerful. Gareth Morgan, a professor at York University in Toronto, Canada, and a consultant on managing change in organizations, has tried to do that. His books *Imaginization* and *Images of Organization* have helped many people break out of the thought prisons to which their lives in the world of organizations have confined them. His message is simple: people cannot develop new ways of organizing themselves to listen and more effectively respond to the challenges they face while working with the images of organization and leadership they have relied on in the past. This means that those of us concerned with church governance must seek to reimagine how people responsible for governing a congregation or other church body might order themselves if they truly seek to listen to God and more effectively carry out their work. Morgan suggests that if we are to really change, we must be willing to suspend our images of what organizations *should* look like and to explore new ways of organizing ourselves to do the critical work before us. He draws heavily on visual images that we do not normally associate with organizations, such as termites and spider plants. His purpose in picking such unusual imagery is to help us shake free of our thought constraints by asking us to look at other ways nature is organized.

One of the most productive times during the 2006 Nashville collegium, which started this research project, was a spontaneous conversation on church organization that began with someone's playful reference to fungi and beetles. The conversation quickly morphed into an exploration of the church as an organic part of a complex ecosystem and the role of discernment. Ecosystems are one of the images Morgan suggests for thinking about organizations. The brain, a machine, an organism, a political system, and a culture are others. But he does not stop there. Morgan also asks us to consider ways in which our organizations might be seen as instruments of exploitive behavior by those outside the organization, psychic prisons to those inside them, or organisms in a continuing state of flux and change. His point, and the point of many others who talk about the need to reframe leadership and organizations, is that we must through new images continually listen and examine our perceptions and what it is we are doing.

I have already shared in chapter 2 the challenges I faced in understanding the paradox of being both servant and leader and my "aha" moment with Jimilu Mason's bronze statue of Jesus. I had a similar "aha" moment in my thinking about organizations. In this case a bowl led to my discovery. I was sitting at my desk preparing to talk to a group of educators about servant leadership and reflecting on Luke's account of Jesus's conversation with his disciples about who was the greatest. Jesus's response caused me to pause for a moment. "The kings of the Gentiles lord it over them; and those who *exercise authority over them* call themselves Benefactors. But *you are not to be like that. Instead, the greatest among you should be like the youngest, and the one who rules like the one who serves*" (Luke 22:25–26, italics added). An innocuous pyramid-shaped organization chart on my desk caught my eye. Many people have used the imagery of an upside-down pyramid to talk about what it means to be a servant, but that day as I rotated the organization chart in front of me 180 degrees so that the top of the pyramid pointed straight down, I made a number of intuitive connections that have continued to feed my imagination. Across the room sat a large clay bowl; I picked it up and turned it over and held it at eye level. The side view of the upside-down bowl looked remarkably like the pyramid, and the bowl, when sitting normally, looked like an upside-down pyramid. The images of a potter carefully shaping a bowl from a lump of clay and the clay basin that Jesus must have used (John 13) when he washed the disciples' feet and admonished them to do the same flashed to mind.

The bowl shape stuck, and I have it used it ever since as a tangible contrast to a pyramid to explore the implications of being a servant and leader in the world of organizations. In addition to using bowls to hold water for foot washing, the church uses bowl-shaped objects to baptize, to serve wine as we celebrate the Eucharist, and to offer water to the thirsty and food to the hungry. We cup our hands to receive and to lift up and let go as we might do with an offering. Each is a bowl-like action. The processes of caring, developing, and sending forth that are so vital in families, communities, and congregations also evoke for me images of hands opened and turned palm up as if to lift and release. The U image in Otto Scharmer's work (discussed in chapter 4) and the holding environment in Ron Heifetz's work (mentioned in chapter 1) evoke similar images.

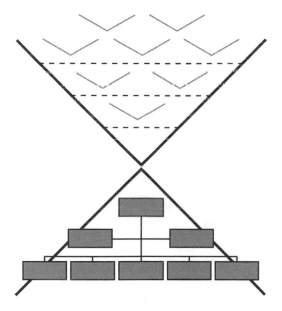

FIGURE 1. BOWL AND PYRAMID

While the bowl imagery has continually fed my imagination, others have been less enamored with it. I remember taking the organization chart of a congregation I was working with and rearranging the boxes used to denote various staff positions, committees, and boards so that the governing board was at the bottom of the bowl. Above the board members were the senior pastor, staff, and other boards and committees. All were arrayed to support the members of the congregation and school in their work both within and outside organization. Above that was the community surrounding the church and school. After rearranging the boxes, I suggested we replace each box with a small shallow V shape to symbolize support and openness. Everyone thought the model helped him or her understand the congregation's ministry better. There seemed to be a genuine excitement in the air about this different way of seeing. On a return visit, however, I noted that the hierarchy and boxes had been restored. When I asked why, I learned that the people in leadership positions were so accustomed to hierarchy that they simply could not get their minds around another way of doing business. They could talk of being a servant, but they couldn't imagine an organization as anything other than a pyramid. Perhaps more disappointing was that the loss of the idea that the governing board and senior pastor were serving the staff, serving their members, and serving the community. The idea that everyone in the congregation was serving the institution had been restored. Sadly, we did not have the opportunity to explore other metaphors that may have helped this particular board get beyond the hierarchical model to which they were so deeply wedded.

The point of this personal narrative about reimaging organizations is not to argue for the bowl as *the* replacement for the pyramid, although I find the bowl an extremely productive image. Morgan suggests dozens of images, any one of which can help open people to different ways of thinking about organizations. These different ways of thinking are essential to our being able to create structures that enable us to be more faithful stewards of the gracious gifts God has entrusted to us. Our challenge is to simply be open to the new things God is doing in our midst, and we can't do that when we are enslaved by images of how people must organize themselves to respond to God's invitations. Our world is continually changing; so must we.

Reimagining Work

How we organize ourselves is closely related to how we perceive the nature of the work we want to accomplish. If the work involves the repetitive offering of well-understood services or the mass production of specific goods, then a pyramid-like organization that has the capacity for control and predictability may be most appropriate. But if we are exploring a new way of doing something or trying to solve a problem we don't yet understand, an organization that encourages freedom and creativity is required. The question facing each organization is, What is ours to do now? Too often organizations do what they do because it's what they have always done and what they know how to do. They recall the old saying that if the only tool you have is a hammer, then every problem becomes a nail. The result is that many governing boards miss the opportunity to do the really important and challenging work they face because it is something they are not used to doing. Ron Heifetz, whose work has been important to many business and government leaders, offers two important insights on work that I believe are important for those interested in church governance. The first is the idea of the holding environment I referred to above. Heifetz defines a holding environment as a place where people gather in a climate of trust to listen and creatively work through the tough issues that their organization faces. Leadership's work is to create and maintain that environment so that people accept responsibility for the work to be done without getting turned off or burned out. I agree, if we understand that the holding environment is foremost a place to listen together, as Scharmer describes the bottom of the U process (chapter 4). Forming a holding environment is not easy work; it requires time, skill, and commitment. But such an environment is essential to understanding and dealing with both the recognized and the unrecognized issues the contemporary church faces. When we do not take time to truly understand what our work is, we miss our potential contribution to our world. My experience suggests that the contemporary church misses much of its potential simply because it does not listen.

The second important insight from Heifetz's work is that there are different types of work. Heifetz views work along a continuum. On one end is work we recognize needs to be done and know how to do. On the other is work that we don't yet understand and have no real idea how to do. The former he calls technical work; the latter, adaptive. In real life, governing work typically involves a mix of both. Knowing the difference and recognizing adaptive work is crucial. Because church governing boards often fail to take the time and accept the risk involved in listening to God and to the people and environment in which they live, they miss much of the adaptive type work that can bring real change in our world. Instead, they wind up spending a good deal of time on the more technical tasks concerned with the finances, facilities, people, and program of the institution. While this work is important and can be challenging, it is not their most important work. Rather, listening together to the needs of people and the world and discerning God's call in the midst of these often competing cries for help are the church's and church governing board's core tasks. Forming and maintaining a viable holding environment create the conditions in which listening can occur. Too often church governing boards push this work off because we don't recognize it or we assure ourselves that it is not our work to do. Folks often say something like, "It's above my pay grade," and refer difficult conversations to some higher authority (including God), thereby holding other people or God responsible for what does or doesn't occur, without recognizing the possibility that they may be the ones who must give voice to needs or pursue a solution.

Real adaptive work requires that people learn together. The task of a governing board and of its leadership in particular is to choreograph and direct a learning process within the board. This is what goes on in the holding environment at the bottom of the bowl described above, as people listen together and form potential responses. Quaker educator and philosopher Parker Palmer uses a series of paradoxes to describe the nature of this space where people can truly listen and learn together. According to Palmer, the space must be bounded and open, emotionally charged and hospitable. It must invite the voice of each person as well as the voice of the group, honor the stories of the people as well as the larger stories of the organization and tradition, support solitude and community, and welcome both speech and silence. Too often our imaginations of governing board life are confined to the current business of the institution. Yes, these things are important, but the amount of attention we devote to them drowns out the larger challenges of listening and learning together that cry out for our attention.

When we continually center governing board life in the institution's day-to-day maintenance, rather than listening, we often miss what Palmer calls "great things." While great things and adaptive work are not synonymous, they both describe challenges that fully engage us in something larger than ourselves. When we miss the great things we could be attending to, we, in Palmer's view, fall out of our "communal orbit into the black hole of posturing, narcissism, and arrogance."[11] The challenge of doing stuff that really matters typically evokes a sense of meaning, community, and creativity that the everyday business of an organization simply cannot.

Why do governing boards spend so little time listening and learning together and devote so much energy to the day-to-day details of administration and maintenance? Participants in this research certainly made clear that we are surrounded with the potential for great things that require creative responses if we but take time to listen. But our ability to sense the possibility of great things is proportional to our capacity for trust, listening, intimacy, vision, healing, learning, and growth. This capacity is essential to creating a truly viable holding environment. It took me a long time to see that in my role as a governing board chair, I was responsible for creating and sustaining a place of trust where people could bump up against ideas from people different from themselves in a climate of listening and inquiry. Once we began to focus on great things and developing trust we were not only able to identify and respond proactively to emerging challenges and opportunities, we were also able to better accomplish the routine work.

What if governing boards were to abandon their fixation on the day-to-day tasks of the organization and to focus on what they might be able to do? Do we have the capacity to imagine great things? Great things are not necessarily large tasks requiring herculean efforts or extraordinary resources. They do not necessarily involve lots of people or strong leadership. Great things can be as simple as the man walking along the beach and throwing starfish back out into the surf. Another person walking on the beach asks him why he's doing what he's doing, because surely he must realize that he can't possibly make a difference. The man replies as he throws another starfish back in, "It did to this one." Great things make a difference in people's lives and in our world. Our calling is to create a holding environment where people can listen to God and to one another, distinguish among the types of work before them, and creatively explore the great things God may be inviting them to undertake.

Reimagining Leadership

Reimaging organizations and reimagining work, especially in a context that seeks first to listen to God, requires that we reimagine the role of leadership in our organizations. Over the past two decades I have sought to imagine what qualities a truly effective contemporary church leader might aspire to. Some have looked at my list of qualities and written them off as unrealistic. They ask, "How could you get anything done if people thought and behaved as you suggest?" Others have looked at this list and wished that they and other church leaders could better embody them. I do not presume to have an inside track on spiritual leadership. These statements come from my experiences as I have sought to discern and live out God's calling and help other individuals and organizations do the same. Those familiar with Henri Nouwen and Robert Greenleaf may recognize their influence, even where they are not specifically cited. The listening servant leader I imagine has the following qualities:

- Is not necessarily called, elected, or employed in a position of authority, but stands simply as her own flawed and vulnerable self, committed to carrying the message that God loves us not because of what we do, but because of who God is
- Values not what society values but seeks to follow the consummate servant leader, Jesus, and measures success by asking, are those served becoming "healthier, wiser, freer, more autonomous and more likely themselves to become servants"?[12]
- Claims irrelevance in the contemporary world as a divine vocation, because it permits him to better understand the anguish and pain present around him and to focus the light of Jesus there[13]

- Understands that the gospel is best communicated to others through relationships built on shared interests, existing circumstances, past experiences, and commitment to service that enable people to encounter the message, especially in times of anxiety and pain, through someone they have come to trust
- Is not simply well informed about the issues that confront her community and world but is also and first rooted in a permanent, intimate relationship with God through Jesus and finds there the source of her words of advice and guidance
- Seeks to claim the time for silence and solitude for himself that Jesus repeatedly sought
- Is called into the community of believers to discover there the presence and power of the Holy Spirit in the many ways the Spirit works
- Understands that she must be a full member of that community, accountable to it, in need of its affection and support, and committed to minister with her whole being
- Needs to be poor, prepared to journey with nothing but a staff (Material wealth can be a tremendous blessing, but being poor and vulnerable offers us the opportunity to see and to hear the needs of our world in ways that possessions or control over resources and wealth do not.)
- Is comfortable with power but chooses to use it to nurture growth in others and their organizations in service to God
- Is so deeply in love with God that he is ready to follow, trusting that he will find life and find it abundantly as he does
- Seeks to listen to others as God listens to our deepest longings and in so doing helps them to disclose and discover their createdness and redeemedness in new ways
- Recognizes that leadership does not rest in one person but in the community as a whole and as the people of that community are gifted and the need requires
- Continually seeks to help prepare others for leadership and to be an effective follower when others are called to step forward

- Knows that while others may entrust her with authority in specific roles, the only real authority she ultimately has is the authority to serve as Jesus served
- Believes that his leadership is finally a matter of stewardship— stewardship of the gospel, stewardship of people, stewardship of the resources that God so richly surrounds and fills us with, and stewardship of a creating creation
- Understands that people serve God in many ways through many organizations and seeks to help each person discover how she can best do that
- Is intimately rooted in the biblical text and the sacraments, viewing them as both familiar and mysterious and as a source of continued wonder and strength, faith and wisdom, hope and promise
- Has faith in the value and meaning of life, even in the face of despair and death, recognizing that every experience holds new promise; every encounter, new insight; every event, a new message

Are these qualities unrealistic in contemporary church governance? There was a time when I would have said yes. The argument that the church needed practical people with experience in leading organizations to successfully govern and administer the affairs of the church was convincing. I no longer think that way. I now believe we need a larger vision of leadership, and we need to reach toward it. I love the oft-quoted and timeless conversation between Alice and the Cheshire cat in Lewis Carroll's *Alice in Wonderland.* Alice asks the wise cat for directions. The cat replies that he needs to first know where she wants to go. When Alice responds that she doesn't much care, the cat tells her that it doesn't matter then which way she goes. Alice's concern is to simply get somewhere, and the cat assures her that she will. So, too, with leadership; not much happens without a dream. If we cannot begin to direct our attention toward something larger than ourselves or our organizations, if we cannot dream about how things might be, we can never change. Jesus asks us to come and follow him. What a wonderful invitation. We need simply to direct our attention toward the Christ whenever and wherever we gather.

We have no way of knowing what will happen when we do so or where it will lead, but we do know that God will be with us every step of the way. That promise feels exciting to me.

Reimagining Meetings

Meetings, too, require reimagination. Church governing boards cannot hope to enhance their capacity to listen to God within a *Robert's Rules of Order* culture. General Robert designed his rules to help groups reach a decision following the parliamentary patterns practiced in the legislatures of his day. *Robert's Rules* have served organizations well by providing a process whereby a group can move forward in an orderly way when people disagree over the best course of action. While *Robert's Rules* permit the voices of all participants to be heard, there is little room for God to speak to the group outside of established parameters. Danny Morris, former Program Director of Developing Ministries at the Upper Room, and Worshipful-Work founder Chuck Olsen, in their book *Discerning God's Will Together*, describe ways our meeting practices limit the church's ability to make decisions and create discordant tones that cannot be resolved with a hymn, prayer, or worship service. In making their case for corporate discernment, Morris and Olsen argue that our attachment to rational thinking, majority rule, denominational policies and procedures, parliamentary rule, and business as usual can all impose limits on our ability to hear God. Even our determination to forge consensus, reliance on personal discernment, and attempts to obey specific scriptures can deflect attention from listening to God together.

How we structure meetings and where we hold them can make a big difference in what goes on in them. I am keenly aware that many church organizations specify in their governing documents how meetings will be conducted. Many boards are also filled with people for whom *Robert's Rules* and denominational practices are sacred. Where this is the case, a little creativity may be required to encourage the group to try out some ways of reimagining meetings. We did several things at Worshipful-Work that could be helpful to governing boards wanting change but saddled with governing documents that require meetings conform to Robert's

Rules or some other established protocol. The first was simply focusing on group discernment; we all felt we needed to know God's invitation. I recognize that the members of the Worshipful-Work board had an advantage that most boards do not: the majority of us had participated in a three-day program on how to restructure meetings around discerning God's desires together. That shared experience was important, but so too was every board member's simple commitment to discernment. While Worshipful-Work no longer exists, Water in the Desert Ministries has picked up where we left off and continues to offer a program on corporate spiritual discernment. Books such as Morris and Olsen's, Steve Doughty and Marjorie Thompson's *The Way of Discernment*, Val Isenhower and Judith Todd's *Listen for God's Leading*, and Suzanne Farnham, Stephanie Hull, and R. Taylor McLean's *Grounded in God* can be a great help.

The way we prepare our meeting space has an effect on what goes on when we meet there. Sitting around a table in a typical church meeting room with the chairperson seated on one end does a lot to reaffirm a business-as-usual atmosphere. When our meeting space permitted, we set up three different areas for our meeting time: one for worship, one for listening to one another and God and discerning God's desire for our ministry, and a third for the business of carrying out God's desires. Our worship space typically centered on an altar or table with a cross, lighted candles, and often bread and wine. The chairs in our listening area were arranged in a circle. The tables in our business area formed a triangle to symbolize the Trinity. Objects such as colorful vases with floral arrangements, small sculptures, icons, pictures, and live plants were included in each area to help keep us centered in God's presence and to appeal to the right side of our brains. When our space was more limited, we sat in a circle with only a low table where a candle and one or more religious objects were placed. Our intent was to always use our meeting space to stimulate our imaginations and keep us centered in worship and listening.

Just as the space for meetings is important, so too are roles that people assume when those meetings occur. The state laws I am familiar with require governing boards to have designated officers.

At a minimum, a president, a secretary, and treasurer are typically required; similar requirements exist in most denomination and congregational governing documents. It does not automatically follow, however, that those same titles and roles need to dictate how meetings are held. When the state of Missouri, where Worshipful-Work was incorporated, required that the organization designate people for specific offices, we simply used two titles, one for our state and federal documents and a second in practice. The president became facilitator; the secretary, scribe; and the treasurer, steward. After a while, we adopted a different approach for the actual conduct of our meetings. We asked various members of our board to serve in one of five roles for each meeting: host, liturgist, keeper of the flame, spiritual guide, and discernmentarian. The host was responsible for making sure that everyone present was comfortable and that our meetings started and ended at agreed-upon times. The liturgist was responsible for developing a specific liturgy for each meeting. Typically, this meant preparing a simple liturgy of scripture, hymn, or poetry that we regularly repeated throughout the meeting, such as the first stanza from the hymn "Breathe on Me, Breath of God": "Breathe on me, breath of God / Fill me with life anew / That I may love what Thou dost love / And do what Thou wouldst do."[14] The keeper of the flame's role was to continually surround the board with silent prayer throughout our meeting. If the person keeping the flame wanted to speak, another board member would assume the role. The spiritual guide listened to the board's conversation, observing how members were responding to one another and to the issue being discussed. The guide's basic role was to view the board's work from enough distance that he or she could help the group sense the Spirit's movement throughout the meeting. The discernmentarian was responsible for guiding the group through its agenda. When further discernment was necessary, the board would typically agree to enter into a time of silence and prayer. If no clear discernment emerged from the time of silence and prayer, the item would be set aside for a time. Occasionally when we faced major issues, the above structure would be set aside, and we would enter together into a time of formal discernment, such as the ten-step process Morris and Olsen outline in *Discerning God's Will Together*[15] One of our board members served as scribe, who recorded all of our deliberations. The scribe's notes served as our official minutes. As the designated board chair, the facilitator, my role was to help the board carry out its work in much the same way as the clerk functions in a Quaker meeting.[16] We planned agendas so that the board focused only on essential issues during our time together and had enough time for silence and reflection while staying within time parameters.

The point of this brief section is not to offer a road map for others to follow but rather to describe a way of meeting as a board that is not based on *Robert's Rules*. Each board should ask itself, How can we better listen to God, one another, and our world and act responsively? The model I have outlined served the Worshipful-Work board well, but it was always a work in progress. We were always open to new ways of being together as a board that would allow us to listen and act while maintaining our original charism. As new members joined and others left the board, we changed and adapted to the new mix of gifts and experiences present. Morris and Olsen point out that as a church, we have allowed ourselves to become enslaved by the way we meet, and that enslavement diminishes our capacity to hear and our ability to creatively respond. That is a shocking indictment, but it is not our fate. We have the capacity to be better stewards of people's talents and become better listeners. Developing that capacity is a simple matter of wanting and being willing to explore and experiment. I'm a great believer in testing things. So often I have watched boards change the way they meet and govern themselves and then submit the matter for a vote. I strongly recommend against that. Instead, try running a test for a year. The time period has to be long enough for people to experience the change and explore the implications of what is changing throughout the whole organization. At the end of the year, evaluate what you have learned and make adjustments. The whole process can be truly energizing for both the board and the congregation.

Reimagining Evaluation

Finally, we must continually evaluate ourselves and our actions. Evaluation is a critical part of life. We grow by continually asking ourselves questions about our thoughts and behaviors, what we are observing around us, and whether our thoughts and behaviors are consistent with God's invitation. This is true for individuals and for organizations. Organizations tend to value data, especially data that is clear, concise, and to the point and that can be objectively evaluated against standards. The most important attributes of community and personal life, however, particularly in the church context, are extremely complex, often "squishy," and not easily quantified. Most information systems are designed to provide hard data about finances, facilities, people, and programs. Since we often can't get solid indicators of progress on seemingly squishy phenomena, we are tempted to limit our evaluation to the questions on which data is easily found. We avoid rough data or stories on the right questions and collect incontrovertible data on less useful issues. This preference for hard data suggests to me that we in the church need to shift our thinking away from the data we collect to how we listen and what we listen to.

For a number of years I was blessed to be associated with Leadership Network, a community of large churches that was founded by former cable executive Bob Buford to help large churches access the resources they needed for their often unique ministries. Bob continually emphasized the need for congregations and other church groups and nonprofits to seek to develop measures of the ultimate effect of their work. These measures of merit typically extend beyond attendance, membership, enrollment, facilities, finances, programs, and worship. They relate directly to what we have discerned God's desires for our congregation or other church organization to be and the effect of what we do on people and the environment. When I first began looking for such measures of merit, I was working with a mainline congregation with an elementary and middle school. Its governing board ultimately settled on three measures where the data could be developed. They labeled the first *lives touched*, which was simply a way of trying to get people thinking about the effect of their presence in the community. With very little effort the board was able to identify approximately five thousand people who had had a significant relationship with congregation and school but were not members or school parents. A second category was *lives changed*. This measure required the governing board to listen to people's stories about how their lives had changed. *Personal ministry of members outside the congregation and school* was the third category. This measure was an attempt to look at how members of the congregation were serving others in a Christ-centered way through their daily lives at work and at home. Some of the information the board collected could be quantified, although most could not, but the simple act of shifting the emphasis from attendance, membership, enrollment, facilities, finances, programs, and worship changed the nature of the conversation within the governing board.

Still, most governing boards I have experience with or knowledge of find it difficult to get beyond the day-to-day business of their organization. Too many believe they don't have the time or capacity on an ongoing basis to collect and evaluate information that cannot be easily quantified. Nor do they believe they have the time or capacity to engage in the critical conversations implicit in focusing their attention on more complex measures of merit. I suspect the deeper reason they don't move beyond the day-to-day is that they choose to avoid the often-difficult conversations that emerge around values and that require real listening to one another. My experience suggests the best way to open a group to listening is through storytelling, and then weaving those stories together into a shared narrative. I remember one especially challenging congregational board that strenuously resisted any activity that was not purely business. I had learned that one older member had been a prisoner of war, and since we were meeting on or very near Veterans Day, I asked him to share something of that experience. To the best of my knowledge, no one else knew of his ordeal. They simply knew him to be a difficult man to be around. But that night—as he told of the fear, cold, and starvation he felt as he made his way west through the devastation and chaos of Germany in early 1945—he began to tear up. Suddenly the group saw a side of him no one knew existed. The members of that board changed that night. They began to share their stories with one another, and as they did, they found that they could begin to talk in a whole new way about a host of issues facing the congregation.

There is more to evaluation than the business of the institution, however. Board members need to look at themselves and how they function as a board. My personal search for a way to better evaluate governing board behavior has led me into a form of examen, or spiritual self-review, that has been a part of Christian spirituality since the earliest days of the faith and was made a part of many lives by Ignatius of Loyola. In her examen of consciousness, Macrina Wiederkehr, a member of the Order of St. Benedict, retreat leader, and spiritual guide, raises questions that guide my sense of how to better evaluate our governing life together. She asks these questions:

> Have we been a good memory in anyone's life today?
>
> Have the ears of our heart opened to the voice of God?
>
> Have the ears of our heart opened to the needs of my sisters and brothers?
>
> Have the eyes of our heart beheld the divine face in all created things?
>
> What do we know, but live as though we do not know?
>
> Have we been a good student of the hours today?
>
> How have we affected the quality of this day?
>
> Have we been blind or deaf to the blessings of the day?
>
> Is there anyone, including ourselves, whom we need to forgive?
>
> When did we experience our heart opening wide today?
>
> Have we worked with joy or drudgery?
>
> Have we waited with grace or impatience?
>
> What is the one thing in our lives that is standing on its tiptoe crying, "May I have your attention please?" What needs our attention?[17]

What if we were to regularly ask ourselves these types of questions individually and collectively during our service on church governing boards? I suspect that many of us would simply blow them off as not appropriate for church governance or something that we simply don't have time to address. But I wonder where our responses might lead us. My experience suggests that our willingness to simply listen to one another and to ourselves is a crucial first step. As we begin to listen, we become more open to the Spirit's movement in our personal and corporate lives and more aware of the possibilities for change and growth and how to best achieve it.

Concluding Thoughts

Each week I give art lessons to a seven-year-old boy. As he paints, we talk a lot about his life and perceptions of the world. My young friend's world and mine are very different, yet for a few hours we share an experience together. He hasn't yet learned how organizations work. He just wants to paint pictures of scenes from around his home that are important to him and his family. My early-childhood-educator friends tell me that every child is an artist until others begin to tell the child he or she is not. The creative edges that make my young friend so wonderfully curious and filled with possibility have not yet been worn down by life in a world obsessed with rational thinking and material things. But I wonder about how those obsessions will shape the quality of the world he is inheriting and the future of the church I hope he will remain a part of.

My fear is that we will continue going about business as usual in our churches, while little by little our already diminished capacity to speak the prophetic voice to the institutions that dominate our society and to see beyond the church's institutional culture is further eroded. We need to step outside the security of our structures, as Turner advocates, and look again at the way we envision and manage our precious time together so that we can see what is really going on in our world and hear God's invitations to respond. This critique is not aimed at those who have so faithfully used their gifts of organization and administration to serve the church; it is instead a warning to us all. We who sit in church governing bodies are out of balance and have allowed our capacity to listen together and imagine to wane. Evidence gleaned from the research for this book makes it clear that many people hunger for a different way of governing within the church. They want to leave their children a more vital church and a better world. If we truly hunger for these things, then we must seek a different way of governing that places listening to God squarely at the center of our being. We need to reimagine our whole way of being the church, beginning with how we govern ourselves. The church is so much more than our current governing models can embrace. My strong desire is to restore wholeness to our governing process and to make listening to God, to others, and to the created world the centerpiece of governing board life. It is this desire that stokes my efforts to reenvision governance. Many others share these desires. Listening to God requires all of us listening and working with all we have—together.

I am writing this final section during the Advent season, when we look longingly toward the birth of Jesus, the long-awaited Messiah, who enters the world not as a conquering hero or skilled governor but as a helpless baby. Many of us are in another kind of advent season, anticipating the birth of a new way of governing ourselves. Like Nicodemus, we hear the invitation to be born again; to set aside the security of established paths of organizing, leading, working, meeting, and evaluating; and to reenter our world transformed in our corporate life. We are invited to become like little children, learners and young artists filled with imagination and wonder, and to humble ourselves, giving up all pretentions of self-importance, independence, self-reliance—all images of how things are or ought to be done—and turning our attention to God. The invocation for the Third Sunday in Advent in Rueben Job and Norman Shawchuck's *A Guide to Prayer* includes the following line: "We beseech thee to make us humble in faith and love, that we may know the joy of the Gospel that is *hidden from the wise and prudent and revealed unto babes*" (italics added).[18] I am able to help my young artist friend learn about colors, the mechanics of drawing, preparing the canvas, and proper care of brushes. I can point out the structure of different trees, the importance of perspective, and a host of other things that experience brings. But he has a freshness and excitement that I no longer have or perhaps never had, and I believe it is this freshness and excitement that the unknown author of this invocation had in mind. As leaders of the church, we are called to regularly proclaim the need to be born again and to become like little children. We are also called to live that message in our governing boards. Our challenge as people in positions of leadership, as congregations, as denominations, or simply as people who care about the kingdom of God and the ministry of Jesus the Christ is to listen together to the Spirit moving in and around us and allow our imaginations of what governance can become to be shaped by that Spirit's leading.

Appendix A

Gender and Professional Classification of Research Participants

	WRITTEN SURVEY							
DENOMINATION	MALE	FEMALE	CLERGY	WOMEN RELIGIOUS	OTHER	LAY	UNDESIGNATED	TOTAL PEOPLE
American Baptist	2	4	5	-	-	-	1	6
Undesignated Baptist	-	2	2	-	-	-	-	2
Southern Baptist	-	-	-	-	-	-	-	0
Christian Church/ Disciples of Christ		1	1	-	-	-	-	1
Church of the Brethren	1	1	1	-	-	1	-	2
Episcopalian	3	3	4	-	-	1	1	6
Evangelical Covenant	-	1	1	-	-	-	-	1
Evangelical Lutheran Church in America	4	1	4	-	-	1	-	5
Lutheran Church— Missouri Synod	1	-	1	-	-	-	-	1
Jewish	1	-	-	-	-	1	-	1
Reformed Jewish	1	-	-	-	-	1	-	1
Mennonite	1	-	1	-	-	-	-	1
No affiliation listed	-	2	1	-	-	1	-	2
Presbyterian Church (USA)	14	7	17	-	1	3	-	21
Reformed Church in America	1	1	2	-	-	-	-	2
Roman Catholic	-	5	-	1	-	4	-	5
Seventh Day Adventist	1	-	1	-	-	-	-	1
Society of Friends (Quaker)	-	-	-	-	-	-	-	0
United Church of Christ	4	1	4	-	-	1	-	5
United Methodist	6	7	9	-	-	3	1	13
Unity	-	2	2	-	-	-	-	2
Total	40	38	56	1	1	17	3	78

NASHVILLE GATHERING

Denomination	Male	Female	Clergy	Women Religious	Other	Lay	Undesignated	Total People
American Baptist	-	1	1	-	-	-	-	1
Undesignated Baptist	-	-	-	-	-	-	-	0
Southern Baptist	1	-	-	-	-	1	-	1
Christian Church/ Disciples of Christ	-	-	-	-	-	-	-	0
Church of the Brethren	-	1	1	-	-	-	-	1
Episcopalian	2	1	1	-	-	2	-	3
Evangelical Covenant	-	-	-	-	-	-	-	0
Evangelical Lutheran Church in America	1	-	1	-	-	-	-	1
Lutheran Church— Missouri Synod	1	-	1	-	-	-	-	1
Jewish	-	-	-	-	-	-	-	0
Reformed Jewish	-	-	-	-	-	-	-	0
Mennonite	-	-	-	-	-	-	-	0
No affiliation listed	-	1	-	-	-	1	-	1
Presbyterian Church (USA)	3	5	6	-	-	2	-	8
Reformed Church in America	-	-	-	-	-	-	-	0
Roman Catholic	1	1	1	1	-	-	-	2
Seventh Day Adventist	-	-	-	-	-	-	-	0
Society of Friends (Quaker)	1	2	-	-	-	3	-	3
United Church of Christ	-	-	-	-	-	-	-	0
United Methodist	2	6	4	-	-	4	-	8
Unity	-	3	2	-	-	1	-	3
Total	12	21	18	1	0	14	0	33

Appendix B

Denominational Affiliation of Research Participants

Denomination	Survey Participants	Nashville Participants	Total Study Participants
American Baptist	6	1	7
Undesignated Baptist	2	0	2
Southern Baptist	0	1	1
Christian Church/Disciples of Christ	1	0	1
Church of the Brethren	2	1	3
Episcopalian	6	3	9
Evangelical Covenant	1	0	1
Evangelical Lutheran Church in America	5	1	6
Lutheran Church—Missouri Synod	1	1	2
Jewish	1	0	1
Reformed Jewish	1	0	1
Mennonite	1	0	1
No affiliation listed	2	1	3
Presbyterian Church (USA)	21	8	29
Reformed Church in America	2	0	2
Roman Catholic	5	2	7
Seventh Day Adventist	1	0	1
Society of Friends (Quaker)	0	3	3
United Church of Christ	5	0	5
United Methodist	13	8	21
Unity	2	3	5
Total	78	33	111

Appendix C

State of Residence of Research Participants

STATE	SURVEY PARTICIPANTS	NASHVHILLE PARTICIPANTS	TOTAL STUDY PARTICIPANTS
Alabama	0	1	1
California	4	0	4
Colorado	2	2	4
Connecticut	1	0	1
Washington, DC	1	0	1
Georgia	1	0	1
Iowa	1	1	2
Illinois	6	0	6
Indiana	5	1	6
Kansas	8	3	11
Kentucky	3	0	3
Massachusetts	1	2	3
Maryland	0	2	2
Michigan	3	2	5
Minnesota	2	0	2
Missouri	8	1	9
North Carolina	2	1	3
Nebraska	2	0	2
New Mexico	0	2	2
New York	6	1	7
New Jersey	2	0	2
Ohio	2	1	3
Oklahoma	1	1	2
Oregon	1	1	2
Pennsylvania	1	0	1
South Dakota	2	0	2
Tennessee	3	7	10
Texas	1	0	1
Virginia	0	3	3
Washington	4	1	5
Wisconsin	5	0	5
Total	78	33	111

Notes

Introduction

1.   Rueben P. Job, *A Guide to Prayer for All Who Seek God* (Nashville: Upper Room Books, 2003), 283.

2.   John Ackerman, *Listening to God: Spiritual Formation in the Congregation* (Herndon, VA: Alban Institute, 2001), 1.

3.   Michael Glaser, *Remembering Eden* (Georgetown, KY: Finishing Line Press, 2008), 12.

4.   Loren Mead, "The Whole Truth about Everything Related to the Church in Twelve Pages (If You Don't Count the Introduction and the Conclusion)" (Herndon, VA: Alban Institute, 1988), xi, xii.

Chapter 1: My Introduction to Church Governance

1.   George A. Lane, *Christian Spirituality: A Historical Sketch* (Chicago: Loyola Press, 1984), 1–7.

2.   Lee Hardy, *The Fabric of This World: Inquiries into Calling, Career Choice, and the Design of Human Work* (Grand Rapids: William B. Eerdmans, 1990), 28.

3.   The Spirituality Wheel is designed to create a visualization of personal and congregational spirituality. The response sheet consists of two circles, each with four quadrants. One circle is for congregational style and one for personal style. The quadrants are numbered 1 through 4. Quadrant 1 is Speculative (mind) Kataphatic (God is revealed), Quadrant 2 is Affective (heart) Kataphatic (God is revealed), Quadrant 3 is Affective (heart) Apophatic (God is mystery), Quadrant 4 is Speculative (mind) Apophatic (God is mystery). Participants are asked to respond to twelve questions about a variety topics, ranging from worship and prayer to concept of God and support of causes, by drawing, in each quadrant, spokes they feel describe them and their congregation. I typically ask participants to post their response sheets, and we talk about what they see.

4. Success Style Profile is designed to help people understand neurological activity and the profound implications thinking style has on their lives. The instrument uses ninety-six forced choice questions around six factors to measure and describe the unique way a person has learned to think while dealing with the everyday challenges of work and life. The six factors include the following:

- *Perception* describes the thinking that occurs in the posterior lobes of the brain as sensory stimulations are transformed into perceptual patterns. Reliance on this factor produces information that is specific, experiential, concrete, detailed, factual, and here and now.
- *Conception* describes the thinking that occurs in the frontal lobes of the brain and that transforms perceptions and previous thinking into relational patterns. Reliance on this factor produces information that is general, intellectual, abstract, "big picture," meaningful, and future focused.
- *Logic, "left-brain" processing*, is influenced by language, which in nearly all cases is handled strictly on one side of the brain. When people rely on left-brain thinking they organize perceptions, solve problems, and make decisions using structure, categories, reason, analysis, calculation, and rules.
- *Feeling, "right-brain" processing*, is influenced by a whole-body response to the world. When people rely on right-brain thinking they organize perceptions, solve problems, and make decisions using feelings, instincts, intuition, hunches, empathy, and values.
- *External attention* takes the form of interaction, communication, performance, involvement, discussion, and influence.
- *Internal attention* takes the form of reflection: memories, analysis, decision making, understanding, feelings, and imagination.

The scoring software program that accompanies this instrument combines these six factors in a number of ways to offer important insights into how people receive, process, and act upon all the information in their life. Individual results can also be combined to produce group profiles.

5. Rick Warren, *The Purpose Driven Church* (Grand Rapids: Zondervan, 1995), 38.

6. Humberto R. Maturana and Francisco J. Varela, *The Tree of Knowledge: The Biological Roots of Human Understanding* (Boston: Shambhala, 1987), 23.

7. Christian de Quincey, *Radical Knowing: Understanding Consciousness through Relationship* (Rochester, VT: Part Street Press, 2005), 28–32. See also Helmut Wautischer, ed., *Tribal Epistemologies: Essays in the Philosophy of Anthropology*, Avebury Series in Philosophy (Burlington, VT: Ashgate Publishing, 1998), 79–115.

8. Helena Norberg-Hodge, *Ancient Futures: Learning from Ladakh* (San Francisco: Sierra Club Books, 1991), xix–xxxii.

Chapter 2: A Vision for Church Governance from the Scriptures

1.   Stephen R. Covey, A. Roger Merrill, and Rebecca R. Merrill, *First Things First: To Live, to Love, to Learn, to Leave a Legacy* (New York: Simon & Schuster, 1994), 218.

2.   David L. Bartlett, *Ministry in the New Testament* (Eugene, OR: Wipf and Stock, 2001), 185–200.

3.   Harry Wendt, *Crossways* (Minneapolis: Crossways International, 2007), 1C–1D.

4.   Brennan Manning, *Reflections for Ragamuffins: Daily Devotions from the Writings of Brennan Manning* (San Francisco: HarperSanFrancisco, 1998), 74.

5.   Robert K. Greenleaf, *Servant Leadership: A Journey into the Nature of Legitimate Power and Greatness* (Mahwah, NJ: Paulist Press, 1977), 49–90.

6.   Gregory F. A. Pierce, *Spirituality at Work: 10 Ways to Balance Your Life on the Job* (Chicago: Loyola Press, 2001), xi.

7.   Parker J. Palmer, *Let Your Life Speak: Listening for the Voice of Vocation* (San Francisco: Jossey-Bass, 2000), 88.

8.   Jill Tabart, *Coming to Consensus: A Case Study for Churches* (Geneva, Switzerland: World Council of Churches Publications, 2003), 1–59.

Chapter 3: Insights for Church Governance from the Book of Nature

1.   During much of the 1990s, I operated a bookstore that sold books on leadership at a discount to clergy and lay leaders. Books by Peter Block, John Biersdorf, Max De Pree, Bill Easum, Robert Greenleaf, Charles Handy, Loren Mead, Gareth Morgan, Chuck Olsen, Peter Senge, Leonard Sweet, Peter Vaill, Margaret Wheatley, and the Drucker Foundation, all of whom understood the importance of science, were perennial best sellers.

2.   Arthur Peacocke, *Theology for a Scientific Age: Being and Becoming— Natural, Divine, and Human* (Minneapolis: Fortress Press, 1993), 216–17.

3.   John Polkinghorne, *Beyond Science: The Wider Human Context* (Cambridge, UK: Cambridge University Press, 1996), 80.

4.   John Polkinghorne, *Science and the Trinity: The Christian Encounter with Reality* (New Haven, CT: Yale University Press, 2004), 12.

5.   Peacocke, *Theology for a Scientific Age*, 35.

6.   Polkinghorne, *Science and the Trinity*, 63

7.   *Nicolaus Copernicus*, Polish astronomer, first theorized that the sun and not the earth was the center of our universe. Twentieth-century astronomers would show further that our solar system lies somewhere amidst billions of galaxies. Many credit Copernicus with beginning the process of objective inquiry into the nature of the world that became science. *Galileo Galilei*, Italian astronomer,

physicist, and mathematician, is credited with inventing the telescope and laying the foundations of modern science, specifically astronomy. Galileo first recognized that time is the appropriate parameter in which to discuss the nature of motion, in particular, falling bodies. *Isaac Newton* developed the idea of time and motion into the notion that the entire universe is a gigantic mechanism following accurate mathematical laws. The industrial revolution brought this level of precision into the day-to-day lives of people who had previously lived in accordance with the natural rhythms observable in nature. *Albert Einstein's* discoveries and formulation of special relativity upset Newton's notion by showing that time was relative rather than absolute. Einstein's name appears on both this list and the one that follows because, while he focused on laws that govern the largest dimensions and energies of physics, his work also opened the door for the development of quantum mechanics (the world inside the atom).

8.   *Niels Bohr*, Danish physicist, made major contributions in understanding the structure of atoms. He first put forth the concept of complementarity; the idea that you could have two mutually exclusive answers to a problem and that both could be right. He also founded the Institute for Theoretical Physics in Copenhagen, which served as a center for theoretical physics in the 1920–30s. English theoretical physicist *Paul Dirac's* formulation of quantum field theory explained how light could be both wave and particle. He also is credited with discovering antimatter. Dirac believed that beauty was a major determinant in the correctness of the mathematical equations describing how the world observed by physics works. *Albert Einstein*, Swiss German physicist, is generally considered the father of modern physics. Einstein revealed that time and space are elastic and capable of changing form, and that they exist in relationship to unfolding life. While Einstein made major contributions to the field of quantum mechanics, he could never accept the randomness and unpredictability of the quantum world. *Werner Heisenberg*, German theoretical physicist, is perhaps best known for articulating the uncertainty principle, which tells us that if we know where an electron is we can't tell what it is doing, and if we know what the electron is doing we cannot determine where it is. Heisenberg and Erwin Schrodinger offered the first fully developed quantum theory. Heisenberg made major contributions to nuclear physics and quantum field theory. *Max Planck*, German physicist, is considered the father of quantum theory. Planck, along with Albert Einstein, was among the first to believe that light had particle-like characteristics as well as wave-like characteristics. In addition to his full development of quantum theory with Heisenberg, *Erwin Schrodinger*, Austrian theoretical physicist, is also known for his famous thought problem of Schrodinger's cat. He shared the 1933 Nobel Prize in Physics with Paul Dirac.

9.   *Classical physics* is the term typically used to refer to the period between the emergence of science based on objective observation of the natural world and the discovery of quantum physics. Definitions of when this period began and how long it lasted differ. I define the period of classical physics here as extending from the discoveries of Isaac Newton, circa 1687, to the publication of Einstein's theory

of special relativity in 1905. Other definitions go back to Copernicus (circa 1515) or Galileo (circa 1610) and extend into the mid-1920s with the acceptance of quantum theory.

10.   *John Dalton*, an English chemist, meteorologist, and physicist, is best known for his contributions to atomic theory. *Michael Faraday* was an English chemist and physicist who made important contributions to our early understandings of electromagnetism. *James Clerk Maxwell,* a Scottish theoretical physicist and mathematician, was the first person to identify light as waves of electromagnetic energy.

11.   Danah Zohar, *The Quantum Self: Human Nature and Consciousness Defined by the New Physics* (New York: Quill/William Morrow, 1990), 24.

12.   From 1971 to 1981 and from 2007 to 2010, *Bill Moyers* hosted the *Bill Moyers' Journal,* a weekly series of conversations about politics and religion, which aired on PBS. His long career in broadcast journalism has included series such as the *Power of Myth, Faith and Reason,* and *Genesis. Krista Tippett* hosts a weekly radio program produced by American Public Media. The show is dedicated to exploring the intersection of religion, meaning, ethics, science, and faith. She has also written two books, *Speaking of Faith* and *Einstein's God. Ira Flatow* hosts National Public Radio's *Science Friday,* a weekly two-hour program of conversations with leading scientists and dedicated to exploring the leading edge of science.

13.   Karen Marie Yust, *Attentive to God: Spirituality in the Church Committee* (St. Louis: Chalice Press, 2001), xxx.

14.   Jim Lochner, "Ask an Astrophysicist," *NASA's Imagine the Universe!* National Aeronautics and Space Administration, http://imagine.gsfc.nasa.gov/docs/ ask_astro/answers/021127a.html.

15.   Paul Butterworth, "Ask an Astrophysicist," *NASA's Imagine the Universe!* National Aeronautics and Space Administration, http://imagine.gsfc.nasa.gov/ docs/ask_astro/answers/971124x.html. Note: Other estimates of the diameter of the universe range up to 156 billion light-years.

16.   This estimate of the length of strings is based on the standard Planck unit of about 10^{-33} centimeters. Planck units, named after Max Planck, are used in describing extremely small subatomic matter. Unlike measurements based on standards such as meters, Planck units are based entirely on natural phenomena.

17.   Albert Einstein first proposed the theory of special relativity in 1905. It changed the way scientists think about space, time, matter, and energy. Most of us are familiar with the equation $E = mc2$; it comes from the theory of special relativity. Special relativity showed time as elastic rather than absolute as classical science believed. Einstein's work sees time curving and warping in response to space, mass, and motion. Ten years after he first published his work on special relativity, Einstein incorporated the effects of gravity, and the theory of general relativity emerged. Gravity slows time. While we don't notice the slowing, it can be measured with highly accurate instruments. Einstein's theories of special and general relativity respectively reconciled electromagnetism and mechanics and offered a new theory

of gravitation and the wave-particle duality of light. While Einstein's discoveries revealed the laws that govern the largest dimensions and energies of physics, his work also opened the world to quantum physics and theories about the existence and nature of black holes in outer space where stars have collapsed and effectively disappeared into a confusing mix of time and space.

18. C. Otto Scharmer, *Theory U: Leading from the Future As It Emerges* (San Francisco: Berrett-Koehler, 2009), 119–21.

19. Krista Tippett, *Einstein's God: Conversations about Science and the Human Spirit* (New York: Penguin Books, 2010), 22.

20. Peacocke, *Theology for a Scientific Age*, 218.

21. Ibid., 218–19.

22. According to quantum theory, the axis of direction for one of a pair elementary particles that have been separated will influence the measurement of its twin. This influence occurs despite physical distance between the two particles and without the knowledge of the people carrying out the experiment. Alain Aspect and his collaborators' experiment referenced here provided strong evidence that a quantum event at one location can affect an event at another location without any obvious mechanism for communication between them. In doing so, they showed that what Albert Einstein, Boris Podolsky, and Nathan Rosen had sought to prove absurd in their EPR (Einstein, Podolsky, and Rosen) paper about quantum physics was indeed the case.

23. Peacocke, *Theology for a Scientific Age*, 35.

24. Zohar, *Quantum Self*, 81.

25. Thermodynamics is the study of energy conversion between heat and mechanical work. Dissipative systems are systems that run down over time. Ilya Prigogine's work with dissipative systems showed that they in fact possess innate qualities that enable them to reconfigure themselves. Until Prigogine's work on the evolution of dynamic systems demonstrated that disequilibrium is necessary for a system's growth, scientists had failed to notice the role positive feedback and disequilibrium played in moving such systems forward. Dissipative systems are resilient rather than stable.

26. The Gaia hypothesis proposes that all the earth's ecosystems and the physical components of its atmosphere, water, ice, rock, soil, and so forth, form a highly complex interacting system that maintains itself in a way that nurtures life as we know it. Disturbing any one piece disturbs the whole. The hypothesis is named after the Greek goddess of the earth, Gaia.

27. Polkinghorne, *Beyond Science*, 122.

28. Polkinghorne, *Science and the Trinity*, 161.

29. Boolean algebra is an abstract mathematical system primarily used in computers to express relationships between sets of objects or concepts. The system permits algebraic manipulation of complicated logical statements to demonstrate their truth by rephrasing them into simpler, more convenient forms.

30.	Polkinghorne, *Science and the Trinity*, 82.

31.	Ibid., 76.

32.	Ann Feild, "Dark Energy, Dark Matter," *Astrophysics—Dark Energy, Dark Matter*, National Aeronautics and Space Administration, http://science.nasa.gov/astrophysics/focus-areas/what-is-dark-energy/.

33.	The number 99.99 appears in a variety of sources; none of them describe how they were derived but all are consistent.

34.	Polkinghorne, *Science and the Trinity*, 76, 80.

35.	Polish astronomer Nicolaus Copernicus's discovery that the earth was not the center of our universe (circa 1543) launched science on a trajectory that steadily pushed humanity away from the center of creation, which theologians had long maintained, into a far less significant role in relation to the vastness of the universe. Over the past few decades, however, scientists have become increasingly aware of how finely tuned the parameters and characteristics of the observed universe must be for carbon-based life, more specifically human life and consciousness, to exist and evolve. Life depends on rather stringent parameters of physical laws that are neither too rigid nor too loose. If they are too rigid, then creation cannot evolve as it needs to. If they are too loose, then there will be no persistence of the forms of life we know. The "Anthropic Principle" recognizes that these parameters exist.

36.	Polkinghorne, *Science and the Trinity*, 76, 80.

37.	John Polkinghorne, *Science and Providence: God's Interaction with the World* (Philadelphia: Templeton Foundation Press, 1989), 38, 45.

38.	Population Division of the United Nations Secretariat, "Percentage living in urban areas by country, definition, graph and map," *Nationmaster.com*, Nation Master, www.nationmaster.com.

39.	Wendell Berry, *The Way of Ignorance and Other Essays* (Berkeley, CA: Counterpoint, 2005), 53–67.

40.	Ibid., 45.

41.	Polkinghorne, *Science and the Trinity*, 73

42.	Wheatley, *Finding Our Way*, 16–31.

43.	Ibid., 21–22.

44.	Diogenes Allen, *Spiritual Theology: The Theology of Yesterday for Spiritual Help Today* (Lanham, MD: Cowley Publications, 1997), 111.

45.	John Polkinghorne, *Exploring Reality: The Intertwining of Science and Religion* (New Haven, CT: Yale University Press, 2005), x.

46.	Peacocke, *Theology for a Scientific Age*, 338–46.

47.	James D. Watson with Andrew Berry, *DNA: The Secret of Life* (New York: Alfred A. Knopf, 2003), 404–5.

Chapter 4: Listening to God

1.	Dallas Willard, *Hearing God: Developing a Conversational Relationship with God* (Downers Grove, IL: Intervarsity Press, 1999), 10.

2. Lon Fendall, Jan Wood, and Bruce Bishop, *Practicing Discernment Together: Finding God's Way Forward in Decision Making* (Newberg, OR: Barclay Press, 2007), 24.

3. Douglas V. Steere, *Gleanings: A Random Harvest* (Nashville: Upper Room Books, 1986), 83.

4. Kurt Lewin, *Field Theory in Social Science: Selected Theoretical Papers* (New York: Harper and Row, 1951), 169.

5. C. Otto Scharmer, *Theory U: Leading from the Future As It Emerges* (San Francisco: Berrett-Koehler Publishers, 2009), 39.

6. Ibid., 39.

7. Willard, *Hearing God,* 10–13.

8. Richard N. Bolles, *How to Find Your Mission in Life* (Berkeley, CA: Ten Speed Press, 1991), 12–14.

9. Val Isenhower and Judith Todd, *Living into the Answers: A Workbook for Personal Spiritual Discernment* (Nashville: Upper Room Books, 2008), 29–33.

10. Willard, *Hearing God,* 29.

11. Ibid.

12. Elizabeth Liebert, *The Way of Discernment: Spiritual Practices for Decision Making* (Louisville, KY: Westminster John Knox Press, 2008), 31–32.

13. Thomas R. Kelly, *A Testament of Devotion* (1941; San Francisco: HarperSanFrancisco, 1992), 9.

14. Richard J. Foster, *Prayer: Finding the Heart's True Home* (San Francisco: HarperSanFrancisco, 1992), 7.

15. Robert Wuthnow, *After Heaven: Spirituality in America Since the 1950s* (Berkeley: University of California Press, 1998), 113.

16. Liebert, *Way of Discernment*, 31.

17. Ibid., 8.

18. Kelly, *Testament of Devotion*, 58.

19. Karen Marie Yust, *Attentive to God: Spirituality in the Church Committee* (St. Louis: Chalice Press, 2001), 16.

20. Jill Tabart, *Coming to Consensus: A Case Study for the Churches*, Risk Book Series (Geneva, Switzerland: WCC Publications, 2003), 15.

21. Ibid., 44.

22. N. Graham Standish, *Humble Leadership: Being Radically Open to God's Guidance and Grace* (Herndon, VA: Alban Institute, 2007), 160–80. What I list as steps here are section headings in Standish's book, which I am directly quoting.

23. Luke Timothy Johnson, *Scripture and Discernment: Decision Making in the Church* (Nashville: Abingdon Press, 1983), 10.

24. Ibid., 109.

25. Leading thinkers from the business world who have impressed on me the importance of listening include John Beckett, Margaret Benefiel, Ken Blanchard, Peter Block, James MacGregor Burns, Tom Chappell, Stephen Covey, Max De Pree, Wilfred Drath, Peter Drucker, Riane Eisler, John Gardner, Bill George, Robert

Greenleaf, Charles Handy, Ron Heifetz, Frances Hesselbein, Dee Hock, Charles Palus, Peter Senge, Peter Vaill, and Margaret Wheatley.

    26.   Kelly, *Testament of Devotion*, 46.

Chapter 5: Voices of Experience

    1.   Water in the Desert Ministries is a nonprofit corporation based in Albuquerque, New Mexico, dedicated to offering opportunities and resources to people seeking a deeper relationship with God.

    2.   Stephen V. Doughty with Marjorie J. Thompson, *The Way of Discernment* (Nashville: Upper Room Books, 2008), 75.

    3.   The nine questions I sent to the seventy-eight participants were as follows: (1) What has drawn you toward the desire to incorporate spiritual practices into church organizational settings? (2) What role have your own spiritual practices played in this beckoning? (3) In what church organizational settings do you find the greatest openness to the integration of spiritual practices and where do you sense the most resistance? (4) What are the foundational issues present that either foster acceptance or lead to resistance to the incorporation of spiritual practices in church organizations? (5) What is necessary to sustain and develop a culture of spiritual practices beyond initial introduction; what limits it? (6) As you look ahead, what movements do you sense in the North American church that will affect the further integration of spiritual practices into organization settings? (7) What joys have emerged for you? What heartaches and disappointments have you experienced? What are your hopes and dreams? (8) What wisdom would you pass on to those seeking to introduce spiritual practices into their organization? What resources would you recommend? (9) In your opinion, what church organizations have been most successful in integrating spiritual practices into their governance? Please name them and, if possible, a point of contact.

    4.   Two hundred sixty-three people who had participated in at least one of the three types of Worshipful-Work hosted events (discernmentarian training, consultant training, and collegiums) offered annually between 1995 and 2001 were initially selected to receive the nine questions. The quotations attributed to participants in this chapter come from original research materials on file with the author and reported on in my Doctor of Ministry dissertation: Donald E. Zimmer, "Listening to God: The Challenge of Deepening Spirituality in the Governing and Administrative Structures of Mainline Denominations " (DMin diss., United Theological Seminary, 2007), 123–54, 190–201, 212–25.

    5.   Urban T. Holmes III, *Spirituality for Ministry* (Harrisburg, PA: Morehouse Publishing, 2002), 83–99.

    6.   Holmes, *Spirituality for Ministry*, 31–32.

    7.   Brian E. Pearson, "Spiritual Direction and the Mysterious Needs of Men," *Presence* 14, no. 4 (December 2008): 10–16.

8. Richard Rohr, *Everything Belongs: The Gift of Contemplative Prayer* (New York: Crossroad, 1999), xxx.

Chapter 6: Imagination

1. Carlo Carretto, "Teach Us to Pray," in *A Guide to Prayer for All Who Seek God*, ed. Norman Shawchuck and Rueben P. Job (Nashville: Upper Room Books, 2003), 300–301.

2. Owen C. Thomas and Ellen K. Wondra, *Introduction to Theology*, 3rd ed. (Harrisburg, PA: Morehouse Publishing, 2002), 260.

3. In his little book *Your God Is Too Small* (New York: Collier Books, 1961), J. B. Phillips cites a variety of images people hold of God, such as resident policeman, parental hangover, grand old man, meek and mild, absolute perfection, managing director, and god-in-a-box, to illustrate how our imaginations restrict our ability to more fully understand God.

4. Avery Dulles, *Models of the Church* (New York: Image Books/Doubleday, 2002), 26–94.

5. Margaret Wheatley, *Finding Our Way: Leadership for an Uncertain Time* (San Francisco: Berrett-Koehler, 2005), 16–31.

6. Peter Block, *Stewardship: Choosing Service over Self-Interest* (San Francisco: Berrett-Koehler, 1993), 13.

7. Riane Eisler, *The Power of Partnership: Seven Relationships That Will Change Your Life* (Novato, CA: New World Library, 2002), xv.

8. Robert K. Greenleaf, *Servant Leadership: A Journey into the Nature of Legitimate Power and Greatness* (New York: Paulist Press, 1977), 13–14.

9. Richard J. Foster, *Prayer: Finding the Heart's True Home* (San Francisco: HarperSanFrancisco, 1992), 102–3.

10. Urban T. Holmes III, *Ministry and Imagination* (New York: Seabury Press, 1976), 134–35.

11. Parker J. Palmer, *The Courage to Teach: Exploring the Inner Landscape of a Teacher's Life* (San Francisco: Jossey-Bass Publishers, 1998), 108.

12. Greenleaf, *Servant Leadership,* 13–14.

13. Henri Nouwen, *In the Name of Jesus: Reflections on Christian Leadership* (New York: Crossroad, 1994), 22.

14. Edwin Hatch, "Breathe on Me, Breath of God," in Shawchuck and Job, *A Guide to Prayer for Ministers*, 83.

15. Danny E. Morris and Charles M. Olsen, *Discerning God's Will Together: A Spiritual Practice for the Church* (Herndon, VA: Alban Institute, 1997), 92–93.

16. Michael J. Sheeran, *Beyond Majority Rule: Voteless Decisions in the Religious Society of Friends* (Denver: Philadelphia Yearly Meeting of the Religious Society of Friends, 1996), x.

17. Macrina Wiederkehr, *Seven Sacred Pauses: Living Mindfully through the Hours of the Day* (Notre Dame, IN: Sorin Books, 2008), 168.

18. Invocation for the Third Sunday in Advent, in Shawchuck and Job *A Guide to Prayer*, 26.

Selected and Annotated Bibliography

Barbour, Ian G. *When Science Meets Religion: Enemies, Strangers, or Partners*. San Francisco: HarperSanFrancisco, 2000. Barbour, one of foremost contemporary thinkers on science and religion, offers a carefully reasoned and highly accessible look at the profound relationship between the creator and creation. In this book he explores astronomy, quantum physics, evolution and continuing creation, neurosciences and human nature, and the character of the relationship between God and nature based on four assumptions. Those assumptions are: (1) science and religion are in conflict with one another; (2) they exist independent of one another; (3) they are separate but in a continuing dialogue; and (4) they are fully integrated and cannot be treated separately. (See also Polkinghorne.)

Beck, Don Edward, and Christopher C. Cowen. *Spiral Dynamics: Mastering Values, Leadership, and Change*. Malden, MA: Blackwell, 2006. Beck and Cowan's *Spiral Dynamics* provides valuable insights into understanding the dynamic forces at work in our personal and communal lives based on learnings in organizational theory and neurobiology. It's a challenging book that has significant implications for the church, which Michael Armour and Don Browning explore in

Systems-Sensitive Leadership: Empowering Diversity without Polarizing the Church. (See also Wilbur.)

Benefiel, Margaret. *The Soul of a Leader: Finding Your Path to Success and Fulfillment.* New York: Crossroad, 2008. Margaret Benefiel has devoted her life to studying and reporting on organizations that are striving to integrate spirituality into their lives. This book is especially important because of the linkages she explores between the threefold path (purgative, illuminative, and unitive) historically associated with personal spiritual journeys and organizational transformation. Benefiel's earlier book, *Soul at Work: Spiritual Leadership in Organizations* (New York: Seabury Books, 2005) also offers important insights on spirituality in organizations.

Block, Peter. *Stewardship: Choosing Service over Self-Interest.* San Francisco: Berrett-Koehler, 1993. Block and Lovett Weems (*Church Leadership: Vision, Team, Culture, and Integrity* [Abingdon Press, 1993]) believe that leadership is stewardship. The notion of leadership as stewardship correlates well with Robert Greenleaf's assertion that the essence of leadership is enabling others to grow and become servants and stewards.

Carretto, Carlo. *The God Who Comes.* Translated by Rose Mary Hancock. Maryknoll, NY: Orbis Books, 1974. In this book Carretto tells of a God who continually comes into a world filled with suffering and open questions and who asks simply that people respond through service. But Carretto calls for more than ordinary church or mission work often entails. He confronts us with the reality that our call may indeed be one of sacrifice. Carretto imposes no guilt; he simply plants the gnawing realization that the walk with Christ is more than the comfortable church lives many of us lead. His works include *I, Francis*; *Letters from the Desert*; and *Why O Lord?*, all published by Orbis Books.

Carver, John. *Boards That Make a Difference: A New Design for Leadership in Nonprofit and Public Organizations.* San Francisco: Jossey-Bass, 1990. Anyone working with church boards needs to be familiar with Carver's policy-based governance model. Of particular value are the twelve very readable guides, published separately by Jossey-Bass, based on this book. Each of the guides focuses on and further develops a separate topic, such as the chairperson's role as a servant, fiduciary responsibilities, assessment, fund-raising, and meetings.

De Pree, Max. *Leading without Power: Finding Hope in Serving Community.* San Francisco: Jossey-Bass, 1997. Max De Pree offers his readers the insights of a seasoned leader who served as the chief executive officer of the Herman Miller Company, an international leader in office furniture manufacturing with annual sales in excess of three quarters of a billion dollars. According to De Pree, the first job of a leader is to define reality, and the last is to say thank you. De Pree is an excellent example of how skillful leadership rooted in deep spiritual values of service and stewardship can succeed in the rough and tumble world of contemporary international business. His first two books, *Leadership Jazz: The Essential Elements of a Great Leader* (New York: Doubleday Currency, 1992) and *Leadership Is an Art* (New York: Dell, 1989) were early cornerstones in my professional life. (See also Steere.)

Dillard, Annie. *Pilgrim at Tinker Creek.* New York: Harper Perennial Modern Classics, 2007. Annie Dillard is in this list of important resources because she notices the dimensions of life that those of us caught up in church governance too often fail to recognize or pass off as insignificant. She helps her readers see holiness in the ordinary of our lives and become more mindful of the smallest and largest reaches of this magnificent creation we have been asked to care for. Other Dillard books that have been especially helpful to me during the writing of this book are: *Teaching a Stone to Talk: Expeditions and Encounters*, *Holy the Firm*, and *The Writing Life*. All are Harper Perennial publications. (See also Polkinghorne, and Intrator and Scribner.)

Doughty, Stephen V., and Marjorie J. Thompson. *The Way of Discernment,* Participant's Book, A Small-Group Experience in Spiritual Formation. Nashville: Upper Room Ministries, 2008. Steve and I served together on the governing board of Worshipful-Work for a number of years, so I was able to observe the development of this book at various points along the way. The book and the accompanying leader's guide authored by Thompson make an excellent stand-alone resource for a group exploring what it is to create a community of discernment. Another useful book is Lon Fendall, Jan Wood, and Bruce Bishop's *Practicing Discernment Together: Finding God's Way Forward in Decision Making* (Newberg, OR: Barclay Press, 2007). (See also Farnham et al., Isenhower and Todd, and Morris and Olsen.)

Doughty, Stephen V. *To Walk in Integrity: Spiritual Leadership in Times of Crisis.* Nashville: Upper Room Books, 2004. Doughty invites people in positions of leadership to reclaim values such as honesty, compassion, simplicity, and humility and to nurture the capacities for joy, lament, and mystery rather than the skills and insights needed to better manage or lead an organization.

Drath, Wilfred H., and Charles J. Palus. *Making Common Sense: Leadership as Meaning Making in a Community of Practice.* Greensboro, NC: Center for Creative Leadership, 1994. Leadership as meaning making was a new idea for me when I first read this book, but it fits well with the images of steward and servant. Drath and Palus believe that people are motivated to engage in any work if it is meaningful to them. The task of a leader then is to help people discover meaning. Howard Gardner's *Leading Minds: An Anatomy of Leadership* (New York: Basic Books, 1995) makes the related point that leadership rests in the ability to relate a compelling story.

Dulles, Avery. *Models of the Church.* New York: Image Books/ Doubleday, 2002. Dulles offers his readers an excellent discussion of five models of the Christian church. They are institution, mystical communion, sacrament, herald, and a community of servants. A balanced view of the church, especially for governance, must include each.

Eisler, Riane. *The Real Wealth of Nations: Creating a Caring Economics.* San Francisco, CA: Berrett-Koehler Publishers, Inc., 2007. In this book, Eisler argues for a new way of establishing economic value that recognizes the importance of caring. She believes that our traditional way of not valuing economically the work involved in the care and nurturing of children, caring for the elderly, and our environment distorts the choices we make in both business and government. Eisler's work is important because it challenges the models we use to establish value and to treat others, and illuminates the unintended human, economic, and environmental consequences of the pursuit of hierarchy and self-service. This book asks people to reexamine the cultural and institutional systems that govern our world and whether the economic calculations that lie at the heart of these systems measure what is truly important in our world. Other books I have found helpful are Eisler's *The Power of Partnership: Seven Principles That Will Change Your Life* (Novate, CA: New World Library, 2002), David Bartlett's *Ministry in the New Testament* (Eugene, OR: Wipf and Stock Publishers, 2001), Betty Sue Flowers *The American Dream and the Economic Myth* (Kalamazoo, MI: Fetzer Institute, 2007), and Walter Wink's, *The Powers That Be: Theology for a New Millennium* (New York, NY: Galilee Doubleday, 1998).

Farnham, Suzanne G., Joseph P. Gill, R. Taylor McLean, and Susan M. Ward. *Listening Hearts: Discerning Call in Community*. Harrisburg, PA: Morehouse, 1991. This little book and a later one jointly written by Farnham and McLean with Stephanie A. Hull, entitled *Grounded in God: Listening Hearts Discernment for Group Deliberations* (Morehouse Publishing, 1999), are enormously practical and packed with valuable insights on discerning God's desires in community. (See also Doughty and Thompson, Isenhower and Todd, and Morris and Olsen.)

Greenleaf, Robert K. *Servant Leadership: A Journey into the Nature of Legitimate Power and Greatness*. Mahwah, NJ: Paulist Press, 1977. This book, together with Robert K. Greenleaf, *Seeker and Servant: Reflections on Religious Leadership*, edited by Anne Fraker and Larry Spears (San Francisco: Jossey-Bass, 1996), and *On Becoming a Servant Leader: The Private Writings of Robert K. Greenleaf*, edited by Don Frick and Larry Spears (San Francisco: Jossey-Bass, 1996), and a host of monographs published by Greenleaf over the years, explores Greenleaf's ideas on what it means to be both servant and leader. Understanding the relationship between the roles is essential for anyone in any leadership role. (See also De Pree, Sims, and Steere.)

Heifetz, Ronald A. *Leadership without Easy Answers*. Cambridge, MA: Belknap Press of Harvard University Press, 1994. Heifetz's discussions of leadership with and without authority, the nature of work, and the essential leadership task of forming and sustaining a holding environment are critical insights for anyone who wants to fully participate in forming and developing their organization. (See also Scharmer and Senge.)

Holmes, Urban T., III. *A History of Christian Spirituality: An Analytical Introduction.* Harrisburg, PA: Morehouse, 2002. This book has been one of the most important books in my library for a long time because of the overview it offers of the diversity in Christian spirituality. Another Holmes book, *Ministry and Imagination* (New York: Seabury Press, 1976), describes the importance of imagination in the church. I found his perspective on the security of the church's structure and the necessity to also move outside it to be especially helpful in understanding the duality I had found in approaches to church governance. (See also Benefiel.) A third book, *Spirituality for Ministry* (Harrisburg, PA: Morehouse Publishing, 2002), examines the spirituality of twenty-two Protestant and Roman Catholic clergy around the University of the South, where Holmes was dean of the School of Theology. Holmes's observations about the clergy he interviewed corroborated much of what I was receiving from the participants in my research.

Intrator, Sam M., and Megan Scribner, eds. *Teaching with Fire: Poetry That Sustains the Courage to Teach.* San Francisco: Jossey-Bass, 2003. I have somewhat arbitrarily selected this book because, without a reference to poetry, this bibliography would not represent the wholeness I believe is essential in organizations. Poetry helps us to see in ways that rational arguments cannot. This book is especially helpful because it includes the works of so many poets, and because of the many parallels between education and spiritual formation. David Whyte's *Crossing the Unknown Sea: Work as a Pilgrimage of Identity* (New York: Riverhead Books, 2001) is an insightful look at the world of work through the eyes of a poet. Judy Brown's self-published *Courage* (Hyattsville, MD: printed by author, 1998) is a wonderful collection of poems written by a prominent business consultant. Poets Wendell Berry, T. S. Eliot, Michael Glaser, Mary Oliver, Rainer Maria Rilke, and William Stafford are also favorites of mine whose work invites us to examine our mental models and to see with new eyes. (See also Dillard.)

Isenhower, Valerie K., and Judith Todd. *Living into the Answers.* Nashville: Upper Room Books, 2008. Val Isenhower, another colleague at Worshipful-Work, and Judith Todd, cofounders of Water in the Desert Ministries, have combined to offer a great resource for someone seeking to discern God's invitation. Isenhower and Todd's book is easy to follow and contains a number of important insights into discernment. Their emphasis on the role of our images of God and how God interacts with humanity is a special contribution to their readers. Isenhower and Todd also have a companion book for people seeking a guide to corporate spiritual discernment, *Listen for God's Leading: A Workbook for Corporate Spiritual Discernment.* (See Doughty and Thompson, Farnham et al., and Morris and Olsen.)

Job, Rueben P., and Norman Shawchuck. *A Guide to Prayer.* Nashville: Upper Room, 1983. This little book and its serial companions, *A Guide to Prayer for All God's People* (1990) and *A Guide to Prayer for All Who Seek God* (2003), have enriched my prayer life and stimulated my imagination for more than a decade. The daily readings from scores of authors are a special treasure of contemplative thought, both ancient and modern. Five other day books have also deepened my journey during the writing of this book. They are *The Book of Awakening* by Mark Nepo, *Bread of the Journey* by Henri Nouwen, *Listening to Your Life* by Frederick Buechner, *I Want to Live These Days with You* by Dietrich Bonhoeffer, and *Reflections for Ragamuffins* by Brennan Manning.

Kelly, Thomas. *The Eternal Promise: A Sequel to a Testament of Devotion.* Richmond, IN: Friends United Press, 1966. Both *The Eternal Promise* and *A Testament of Devotion* (San Francisco: HarperSanFrancisco, 1992) were compiled from Kelly's writings following his early death. Each has been important to me at a different time in my life. The two books explore what contemplative living means in our contemporary society and the fundamentals of the Quaker perspective on faith and life.

Liebert, Elizabeth. *The Way of Discernment: Spiritual Practices for Decision Making.* Louisville, KY: Westminster John Knox Press, 2008. If I had one book to read on discernment that embraced both its practical and its theoretical dimensions, this would be it.

Discernment, as Liebert sees it, involves listening with one's whole being in the context of community and the created world, and she walks her readers through each part in a highly understandable and useable way. (See also Doughty and Thompson, Isenhower and Todd, Morris and Olsen, and Vennard.)

Lindahl, Kay. *Practicing the Sacred Art of Listening.* Woodstock, VT: Skylight Paths, 2003. This book is a very practical guide to enhancing our capacity to listen to one another in a variety of settings. In her view, listening is an art and a precious gift that transforms relationships. Lindahl stresses the importance of choosing to listen and developing the opportunities to do so. (See also Steere, *On Listening to Another.*)

Morgan, Gareth. *Images of Organization, the Executive Edition.* San Francisco: Berrett-Koehler, 1998. This book and Morgan's earlier work *Imaginization: New Mindsets for Seeing, Organizing, and Managing* (Berrett-Koehler) are intended to help expand our perceptions of leadership, authority, and organization. Thomas Sergiovanni's *Moral Leadership: Getting to the Heart of School Improvement*, which offers an insightful discussion of the sources of authority, and Ron Heifetz's material on leading with and without authority in *Leadership without Easy Answers* should also be read.

Morris, Danny E., and Charles M. Olsen. *Discerning God's Will Together: A Spiritual Practice for the Church.* Herndon, VA: Alban Institute, 1997. Morris and Olsen's book was my introduction to spiritual discernment, and as such it will always occupy a special place in my treasury of resources. At the book's core is an easily understood ten-step corporate discernment process that has been used widely within a variety of denominations. Many of the people who participated in my research began their work to transform church boards with this discernment process or a version of it. (See also Doughty and Thompson, and Isenhower and Todd.)

Nouwen, Henri J. M. *In the Name of Jesus: Reflections on Christian Leadership.* New York: Crossroad, 1994. In this book, Henri Nouwen describes his vision of what a Christian leader of the future is called to be. Nouwen talks about leaders who are vulnerable, poor, irrelevant, powerless, and humble. He stresses the importance of seeking to know the heart of God as made flesh in Jesus, ardently desiring to be in God's presence, and trusting that God is at work in each of us to move us to the inner and outer places that God desires. He believes that leaders must be moral, mystical, and fully equipped to discern the Spirit of God's movement. In a few simply and poetically written pages, Nouwen brings Greenleaf's servant model into the center of Christian life. Other Nouwen books—among them, *Can You Drink the Cup?, Life of the Beloved, Out of Solitude*, and *The Return of the Prodigal Son*—have especially nurtured my spirit and thought.

Olsen, Charles M. *Transforming Church Boards into Communities of Spiritual Leaders.* Herndon, VA: Alban Institute, 1995. This groundbreaking book helped launch a continuing movement to change the way church boards and committees work. Olsen reports on his research into how people felt about their service on church boards and proposes an alternative that is built around a continuing process of biblical and theological reflection, personal and communal storytelling, weaving of narratives, reflecting on their meaning, communal discernment, and envisioning a new future.

Palmer, Parker J. *A Hidden Wholeness: The Journey toward an Undivided Life: Welcoming the Soul and Weaving Community in a Wounded World.* San Francisco: Jossey-Bass, 2004. The body of Palmer's work emphasizes the importance of wholeness, call, servanthood, and social activism. This book and *Let Your Life Speak: Listening for the Voice of Vocation* (Jossey-Bass, 2000) challenge readers to seek their calling and align their life to it. *The Courage to Teach: Exploring the Inner Landscape of a Teacher's Life* (Jossey-Bass, 1998) and *The Active Life: Wisdom for Work, Creativity, and Caring* (San Francisco: HarperSanFrancisco, 1990) are also important resources. The former was written primarily to help teachers recover the spirit that initially brought them into teaching. I mention the book here because the Courage to Teach program it spawned has since been expanded to include clergy. *The Active Life* reflects Palmer's belief that a spiritual life is lived not within monastic settings but in the day-to-day world.

Phillips, J. B. *Your God Is Too Small.* New York: Collier Books, Macmillan, 1961. It was the title of this book that first caught my eye. In Phillips's view, the more we try to define God, the smaller God becomes. He cites a number of images that he believes diminish God, then lists others that he believes offer a more adequate view of God. Phillips believes we can never have too big a concept of God. As science tells us more and more about the scope and detail of creation, our concept of God needs to grow. But while God exceeds our abilities to conceptualize, God is also present to us in the human form of Jesus and his life, death, and resurrection.

Polkinghorne, John. *Exploring Reality: The Intertwining of Science and Religion*. New Haven, CT: Yale University Press, 2005. Polkinghorne has been a physicist, theologian, and college president. He is, in my estimation, one of the leading thinkers about the nexus of science and religion and his books are a must-read for anyone seeking to gain a better understanding of God and creation. Polkinghorne's work makes the world inside the atom more accessible to church leaders and is mandatory reading for anyone seeking to better understand the wonders of creation. Altogether I used nine of his books in my research for this book. Each deals with a slightly different aspect of the relationship between science and Christianity. Three of them deserve special mention. They are *Quarks, Chaos, and Christianity: Questions to Science and Religion* (1994), *Science and the Trinity: The Christian Encounter with Reality* (2004), and *Quantum Physics and Theology: An Unexpected Kinship* (2007). Arthur Peacocke's *Theology for a Scientific Age: Being and Becoming—Natural, Divine, and Human* (Minneapolis: Fortress Press, 1993) is another book I found quite helpful in understanding the relationship between science and religion. Both Polkinghorne and Peacocke are scientists of considerable academic stature and Anglican clergy. Sam Kean's *The Disappearing Spoon* offers highly readable insights on the periodic table that can be a great help in understanding how the world inside atoms translates into the metals, gases, and liquids that make up the world we are more familiar with.

Rohr, Richard. *Everything Belongs: The Gift of Contemplative Prayer*. New York: Crossroad, 1999. Early in his book Rohr makes the point that we cannot come to know God or fabricate a moral response to God solely in our heads. We can only begin to know God when we agree to bear the mystery of God, and we can only come to bear the mystery of God when we lay aside all the elements of life that clutter and distort our ability to see and understand what is ours to do. Our challenge is to learn to live in the now, not in compliance with a set of rules but out of a deep relationship with God.

Scharmer, C. Otto. *Theory U: Leading from the Future As It Emerges*. San Francisco: Berrett-Koehler, 2009. Scharmer's unique contribution to those of us who serve in governing roles is his careful articulation of the need to deeply listen together to one another and our world and then to act appropriately. Both listening and acting are necessary; the issue is what level of listening is required. Scharmer believes we must develop the capacity to listen together with openness to what has not yet emerged in our individual and collective consciousness. In his view, action rooted in this type of listening together results in a more timely and focused response than would otherwise be possible. The in-depth listening together Scharmer describes correlates with Heifetz's understanding of the nature of listening required for adaptive work and the type of listening generally associated with corporate discernment. (See also Heifetz and Senge.)

Senge, Peter, Richard Ross, Bryan Smith, Charlotte Roberts, and Art Kleiner. *The Fifth Discipline Fieldbook*. New York: Currency Doubleday, 1994. Peter Senge has been responsible for a number of important books about the creation of learning organizations. I have singled out *The Fifth Discipline Fieldbook* because it is easy to understand and use. The five disciplines Senge and his coauthors believe are essential to creating organizations that can learn and adapt are as follows: personal mastery, mental models, shared vision, team learning, and systems thinking. The practices of these disciplines evidence an environment where people are committed to personal growth, continually question the mental models of reality they hold, share a sense of purpose and direction, willingly learn together, and continually work to see what they are doing as a part of a larger whole. (See also Heifetz and Scharmer.)

Sims, Bennett J. *Servanthood: Leadership for the Third Millennium*. Cambridge, MA: Cowley, 1997. In this book Sims challenges his readers to look at what it means to be servants to one another in a world that seems irretrievably caught up in the pursuit of power and the willingness to exploit both the creation on which we depend and the people with whom we share life. Sims translates Greenleaf's theory into the day-to-day theological and programmatic choices we make. This book and the offerings of the Servant Leadership School of Greensboro founded by Sims can be enormously valuable to any person or organization seeking to live the life of a servant in contemporary North American society.

Steere, Douglas, V. *On Listening to Another*. New York: Harper Brothers, 1955. Steere entered my life through an unattributed quote on listening that someone gave me. In Steere's view, to give one's undivided attention to another so as to better understand that person is a gift of inestimable value. E. Glenn Hinson's biography of Steere, *Love at the Heart of Things*, and Steere's *Gleanings: A Random Harvest* (Nashville: Upper Room, 1986) and *God's Irregular: Arthur Shearly Cripps; A Rhodesian Epic* (London: SPCK, 1973) offer valuable insights into the life of an enormously gifted Quaker who lived a contemplative life on the world stage throughout the twentieth century. He worked for peace and interreligious dialogue and helped people caught in a myriad of conflicts and their aftermath. (See also De Pree.)

Steindl-Rast, David. *Gratefulness, the Heart of Prayer: An Approach to Life in Fullness*. New York: Paulist Press, 1984. Prayer is essentially an act of gratitude. Steindl-Rast believes even the most ardent plea for healing comes out of our final acceptance that we are utterly dependent on God. Giving thanks in all things means that we have submitted our whole selves to God's purpose. When we are able to become grateful for life as it is, we are able to listen more attentively and be more open to God working through us in surprising and profound ways.

Tabart, Jill. *Coming to Consensus: A Case Study for the Churches*. Geneva, Switzerland: World Council of Churches, 2003. Tabart tells the story of the Uniting Church in Australia's efforts to find a better way of dealing with contested issues and discerning a path to move forward. This small book provides an excellent description of cultural change process within a denomination.

Underhill, Evelyn. *The Spiritual Life*. Harrisburg, PA: Morehouse, 1955. Underhill's little book describes the true nature of a spiritual life. She believes that a true spiritual life is not some extreme form of existence but a life lived as an open channel for the desires of God's heart for this world. A spiritual life is a life lived from the center outward. It is not a life rooted in what we need or want but in being fully present for God.

Vennard, Jane E. *A Praying Congregation: The Art of Teaching Spiritual Practice*. Herndon, VA: Alban Institute, 2005. Vennard's book is an invaluable resource in helping people learn to pray. Throughout my book I have emphasized the importance of governing boards listening together. I would start that process with this book. Vennard makes communicating with God come alive in ways that few authors have been able to approach.

Wilbur, Ken. *The Integral Vision: A Very Short Introduction to the Revolutionary Integral Approach to Life, God, the Universe, and Everything*. Boston: Shambhala, 2007. Wilbur's life's work has been to try to understand how everything fits together. His work can be complex, but this book does an excellent job of summarizing his core ideas. I have found his description of spirituality and parallel comparison of various theories of human and societal development to be quite helpful.

Willard, Dallas. *Hearing God: Developing a Conversational Relationship with God*. Downers Grove, IL: InterVarsity Press, 1999. Willard's message is that it's not about what decisions we make or what actions we take; rather, our emphasis needs to be developing and maintaining a personal relationship with God, because through such a relationship we can best know the desires of God's heart. This insight has been critical in my journey to discern and live out my personal calling, and I believe it applies equally to organizations of all types. Luke Timothy Johnson's *Scripture and Discernment: Decision Making in the Church* (Nashville: Abingdon Press, 1983) is another valuable resource. Johnson's premise is simple: there ought to be a connection between the way we go about the business of the church and the church's claims to be a community of faith seeking to follow the Spirit's leading.